Shopping & ~~~~

Calais

Boulogne, Dunkerque & Le Touquet

© 2003 by Passport Guide Publications
19 Morley Crescent, Edgware HA8 8XE

Written By:	Sharron Livingston
Published By:	Passport Guide Publications
Enquiries :	Tel: 020 8905 4851
	Fax: 020 8933 4307
Email:	Sharron@channelhoppers.net
Web site:	www.channelhoppers.net

ISBN: 1-903390-01-X

- 130 shops
- 2 hypermarkets
- 20 restaurants
- an under surveillance covered car park
- 4 150 spaces available
- a filling station opened 24 hours a day

www.cite-europe.com

Be an adventurer, go across the Channel to have the largest choice !

Motorway A 16 Exit 12 & 14

Carrefour

Contents

Carrefour Cité Europe

Everything you need under one roof

Usual opening hours
From 9.00am till 1000pm Monday to Friday
From 8.30am till 10.00pm Saturday
Closed on Sunday

Special opening hours
From 9.00am till 8.00pm
Monday April 21st
Thursday May 29th
Monday June 9th
Friday August 15th
Saturday November 1st
Tuesday November 11th
Sunday November 23rd
Sunday November 30th
Sunday December 7th
Sunday December 14th
Sunday December 21st

Carrefour Cité Europe
1001 Boulevard du Kent
62231 Coquelles
Tel: 00 44 (0) 321 46 75 55
Fax: 00 33 (0) 321 46 75 57
Web: cite-europe-carrefour.fr

Show this voucher at the information desk with your till receipt

Carrefour Cité Europe

to receive a
15€ gift voucher for every
200€ spent in the shop
(excludes petrol)

Name.................................
Surname:...........................
Address:.............................

....

....
E-Mail:...............................

Contents

Introduction

Shopping and Leisure, What a Pleasure!

I must have crossed the Channel to Northern France at least 300 times in the last seven years, yet I still enjoy my stays there as much as ever and always find something new to enjoy.

The joys of Calais are well published and as long as the British are being taxed into sobriety, this industrial coastal town will remain a popular bargain shopping destination.

Every year, millions of Brits cross the Channel in search of bargain wine, beer, spirits and a host of other practical products from cooking pots to washing machines. The fact that there are four operators crossing this short 26 mile stretch of the English Channel between Dover and Calais is testament to the popularity of the bargain.

However, just fifteen minutes by car from Calais, a beautiful coastal land-scape unfolds harbouring a clutch of sleepy fishing villages with small hotels and rustic restaurants which offer insights into rural France.

A twenty minute sprint on the motorway takes you to picturesque Bolougne. Add another twenty five minutes to your journey to get to the highly elegant, wonderfully manicured resort of Le Touquet where shopping is stylish and architecture takes on an art form.

Even Dunkirk has been redevekioed offering visitors a chance to review their perceptions of the town as merely a former war zone. Of course the history is still an essential part of Dunkirk, but the area has been revamped to create a pleasurable short break destination.

Vive La Short Break.

Sharron Livingston

Introduction

Meet the team at this year's Channel Hopper's Guide Wine Tasting

Left to right: Richard Bampfield MW, Anthony Rose, Deborah Collinson, Casper Auchterlonie, Caroline Bosworth-Davies.

Richard Bampfield MW has spent most of his working life managing wine businesses while becoming a Master of Wine. Richard is now an established wine consultant, educator and judge. He is also an experienced 'Bon Vivant' whose expertise at wine events is greatly sought. **www.winevents.co.uk Tel: 01628 638131**

Anthony Rose is wine correspondent of The Independent, a contributor to Wine Magazine, Decanter, Harpers, Winepros.com and has co-authored the annual wine guide, Grapevine. He teaches wine at Leith's School of Food & Wine and judges wine competitions around the globe. He won the Glenfiddich & Lanson Black Label Wine Writer of the Year awards and the Lanson Champagne Writer of the Year 2002 award.

Deborah Collinson runs her own media relations company specialising in the wine trade. She is a wine writer, an experienced judge at international wine competitions and organises the most prestigious award for wine writers, Le prix du Champagne Lanson. **Tel: 020 7373 0774**

Casper Auchterlonie is a wine merchant, a wine writer and a regular contributor to Wine Magazine, Wine & Spirit International and many other wine publications. He is an established wine judge, wine lecturer, wine consultant and holds corporate wine tastings. **www.littleredbottle.com**

Carolyn Bosworth-Davies has worked in the wine trade for over 20 years. She is a freelance wine writer and educator specialising in wine appreciation courses in South East London and enjoys enthusing her audiences about wine and its diversity through wine tastings and events. She is currently chairman of the Association of Wine Educators. **www.wine-educators.com Tel: 020 8931 1128**.

Hopping Over

The perks of shopping abroad start on board where products are available at low French duty paid prices.

Crossing	From/To	Journey Time	Frequency
Hoverspeed: Seacat Tel: 08705 240 241 www.hoverspeed.com	Dover/ Calais **Check-in:** 30 mins	60 mins	11 sailings daily
Eurotunnel Tel: 0990 353535 No foot passengers. Vehicles only. www.eurotunnel.com	Folkestone/ Calais Turn up **Check-in:** 20 mins	35 mins	Every 15 mins peak time
P&O Ferries Tel: 0870 20 20 20 www.POferries.com	Dover/ Calais **Check-in:** 30 mins	75 mins	Every 45 mins peak time
SeaFrance: Tel: 0990 711711 www.seafrance.com	Dover/ Calais **Check-in:** 45 mins	90 mins	Every 90 mins peak time
Norfolkline: Tel: 0870 870 1020 www.norfolkline.com	Dover/ Dunkirk **Check-in:** 60 mins	120 mins	6 times a day peak time

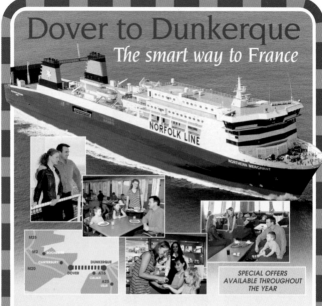

Calais Town

Calais is the closest French port to England and the evident touristic appeal centres around shopping. But is that all Calais has to offer?

Having suffered the ravages of war, Calais was completely rebuilt after World War II. Most people now see this port as a lattice-work of commercial streets, conveniently located solely to enjoy the benefits of cheaper shopping. Right?

Well, maybe not. Its well established cross-Channel links and geographical location makes it a good starting point to many destinations. The motorway network via the A26 and A16 means easy journeys to Belgium, Strasbourg, Paris, Germany and of course the rest of France.

But those staying a while will see that Calais is really three towns in one: Calais-Nord, Calais-Sud and Calais-Ouest. Calais-Nord is the harbour area and is home to **rue Royale**, considered to be the one of the smarter shopping streets. It also boasts the smartest restaurants. Calais-Sud is the main town centre with a variety of shops and department stores. Calais-Ouest is where the Cité Europe shopping complex is located. Its ultra-modern building contrasts sharply with the nearby ruined fortifications.

How to Get From the Port to the Town Centre

Follow the **Toutes Directions** sign. At the roundabout take the fourth exit sign-posted **Centre Ville**. Turn left at the next roundabout, drive along the canal and at the traffic lights turn right. This leads to the square in front of the Town Hall with Calais-Nord to your right and Calais-Sud to the left. Turning right leads you to the seafront, rue Royale and Place d'Armes.

Calais Town

Aside from its commercial aspect, the Calais area has a varied range of leisure activities. The vast sandy beaches are popular with both the locals and tourists. There are numerous activities on offer such as sailing, sail boarding, speed sailing, sand yachting, water skiing or just plain sun bathing.

It generally comes as a surprise to first-time visitors, but the surrounding area's beautiful countryside is ideal for a leisurely stroll, off-road cycling, horse riding and even fishing.

And if all of this is too much, you can always take one of the canal cruises along the waterways that criss-cross the Marais Audomarois and contemplate your next shopping trip!

Cycle Hire
VTT Brame Sports
178 Boulevard la Fayette
Calais

Canal Cruises
Marais Audomarois
Nature Park Audomarois
Tel:00 33 (0) 321 98 62 98

La Grange Nature de Claimarais
Tel: 00 33 (0)321 95 23 40
Fishing,, rowing boats, boat trips and canan ('watergang') cruises.

Offshore Cruises
For information about sailing down the Côte d'Opale on the yacht Ophelie to Cap Blanc-Nez
Tel: 00 33 (0)231 93 63 71
or contact the tourist office.

Riding
Cheval Loisir
182 route de Gravelines
Calais
Tel: 00 33 (0)321 971 818
Escorted countryside rides.

Water Ski
Le Club de la Gravière
Bleriot-Plage
Tel: 00 33 (0) 321 34 63 50

Calais Sights

Take in a few sights while in Calais. After all it was under English rule for more than 200 years during the occupation of 1347-1558.

Hôtel de Ville, place du Soldat Inconnu

One of Calais' finest landmarks is the Town Hall which can be seen for miles. This magnificent Flemish-style structure built of brick and stone, was completed in 1925 and dominates the main square. It houses many paintings and is adorned with stained-glass windows which tells the story of the departing English. It also serves to diffuse the sunlight around the grand staircase. The interior is renowned for the elaborate decor of the reception rooms. Also attached to the town hall is an ornate brick clock tower and belfry which stands 74m/246ft high. The chimes of its bells are most appealing. Visiting hours 08.00-12.00 and 13.30-17.30

Rodin's Six Burghers place du Soldat Inconnu

At the foot of the clock tower and Town Hall stands Rodin's original 19th-century live size bronze statue of the Burghers of Calais. The bronze work, consists of six statues recalling the final year of the Hundred Years War. The mayor, along with other prominent citizens assembled here wearing only their shirts, before surrendering to King Edward II. They were willing to sacrifice their lives to save Calais from being massacred by Edward at the end of his six-month siege.

Les Six Bourgeois de Calais

The Town Hall. Inset : Rodin's Burghers

Their heroism moved the King's French wife, Philippine of Hainault, sufficiently to plead successfully for their pardon.

Take a moment to examine each statue. Notice the veins and the clenched muscles, and the tension in their torsos, betraying their proud apprehension at their imminent humiliation.

Parc St. Pierre

The well tended park opposite the town hall offers an idyllic setting for summer picnics . The statue in front of the park is **Monument du Souvenir**, a memorial to the unknown soldier.

Musée de la Guerre

In the middle of the Parc Saint Pierre is an old camouflaged German bunker. It was once a telephone exchange during the World War II, but today serves as a war museum. Inside there are posters, old war-time documents and memorabilia together with historical recollections of the Resistance, Calais' occupation and the Battle of Britain. The war museum is open daily from 10.00-17.00 from February to December. Entry fee is around £1.50.

The Tourist Office
21 Boulevard Clémenceau
BP 94 62102, Calais
Tel: 00 33 (0)321 96 62 40

General Market Days
Place de Crève Coeur,
Place d'Armes
Wed, Thurs, and Sat. am.

Annual Brocante August 16
350 "bric à brac" stalls make this the largest summer street market.

Did You Know..

that both Emma Lyons (Nelson's Lady Hamilton) and Beau Brummell sought refuge from creditors in Calais. Lady Hamilton died in Calais at 27 rue Française in 1815 poverty-stricken and thoroughly miserable.

A year later Brummell made his way here to avoid his creditors and the displeasure of his former friend the Prince Regent. During his 15-year stay he was known by his first two names George Bryan.

Citadelle
nr Square Vauban

Dating back to 1560 this was originally built to house the town's garrison after the French retook Calais. Much of the later work is attributable to the French engineer Vauban. Today it is used as a sports centre.

Place D'Armes

Once upon a time, this was the main bustling area of medieval Calais. Alas, war-time devastation destroyed most of the original square leaving just a 13th- century watchtower as a reminder of this time. This popular square, just a short walk away from the harbour and some fine restaurants, is surrounded by cafés and shops. Three times a week, the car park in the middle turns into a colourful general market.

Eglise Notre-Dame,
rue Notre Dame

The architecture of the church is partly English Gothic in style, a legacy of English rule between 1347 and 1558. In 1921Captain Charles de Gaulle married a local girl called Yvonne Vendroux here.

Musée de Beaux Arts et de la Dentelle
25, rue Richelieu

The Museum of Fine Art and Lace houses paintings from the 15th to 20th century and sculpture from19th and 20th century. On display are exhibits of Calais' lace - an industry originating from England. Incidentally the first lace factory was established in Calais at **rue de Vic** in the URSSAF building. The museum is open Wednesday to Monday 10.00-12.00 and 14.00-17.30. Entry £1.50.

Did You Know.. that the beach at Blériot-Plage (just before the D940 coastal road) is named after the inventor Louis Blériot. He was the first man to cross the channel in a flying machine that was heavier than air. He flew his monoplane from this spot 1909.The annual Blériot Air Show, a tribute to Louis Blériot, is quite an extravaganza of air display and aerobatics. Further information from Sangatte-Blériot-Plage Tourist Office Tel: 00 33 (0)321 34 97 98.

Calais Insights

Take a walk along Rue Royale and enjoy some unusual shopping.

If you like to dine from fine porcelain, drink from crystal and adorn your home with fine decorative designer items, here is a tip: stylish Lalique and Baccarat crystal, items made by Christophle, porcelain from Royale de Limoges and Versace dinner sets are available at **René Classe** at 61 Rue Royale. They cost between 20-33% less than normal UK prices! For instance a Villeroy & Bosch 26cm dinner plate costs £12.34 here and £23.40 in the UK and a Lalique Crystal Bacchante costs £1,579.16 here and £1,999 in the UK!

Anyone for tea? Around 70 varieties can be purchased at **Brulerie La Tour** at 65 rue Royale. In fact e verything you could wish for to enjoy a cuppa is available on their shelves including pretty tea sets and a range of tempting chocolates and and biscuits.

Au Royal Chocolat at number 67 is a quaint chocolate shop. On sale is '**Les Coucougnettes**' awarded the 'Best Speciality Sweet in France' by the Salon International de La Confiseries Paris. They were enjoyed by King Henry IV and If you too like marzipan, you will love them. A bag of **Les Coucougnettes** costs £6.90. Also on sale are a range of Daskalides Belgian chocolates. You would never know it, but they are sugar free! 100g costs around £1.90.

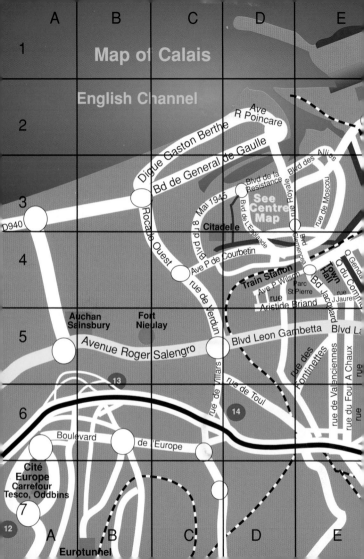

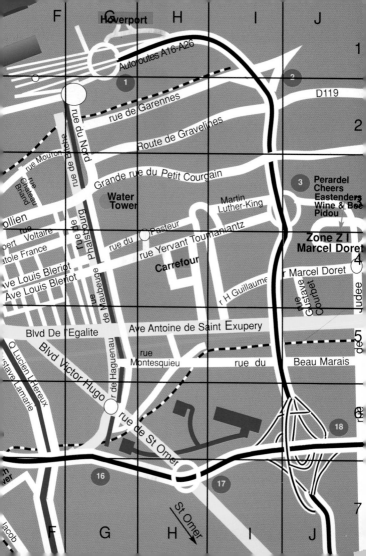

As with all trips, your journey starts in transit, whether by train or boat.

Those 26 miles that lie between Dover and Calais provide the cross-Channel operators with an audience of potential shoppers and wisely they provide their customers with bargains either on board or in outlets in their passenger terminals.

This year we invited them to submit samples to our wine tasting. Three responded. Euroshop tends to favour French wines whereas P&O Ferries and Hoverspeed are more global in their approach. This is a review of their samples.

Euroshop
Eurotunnel Terminal
Coquelles
Tel: 00 33 (0)321 00 47 16

English:	Yes
Tasting:	Promotion wines only
Payment:	£, 💳 💳
Parking:	Yes
Open:	24/7

The Euroshop, situated within Eurotunnel terminal, is ideal for those travelling with Eurotunnel who still have an empty boot.

The wine range is predominantly French with some fine wines on offer, complemented by some Australian, American and South African wines.

Recommendations

Freixenet Cava £42.25
An easy to drink bottle of Spanish fizz.

Chateau Mondotte-Bellisle Saint Emillion 1998 £7.08
1998 was a terrific vintage for Saint Emillion, and this is full flavoured and rounded. Drinking well over the next couple of years.

Hoverspeed
Calais Terminal and
on board the Seacat
Tel: 01304 865000

Map Ref: G1
Bus No:
English: Yes
Tasting: Promotion wines only
Payment: £, 💳 💳
Parking: Yes
Open: Daily

Those travelling with Hoverspeed will have the opportunity to make purchases at their shops on land and on board. Order on board and take advantage of their select and collect service: your goods will be packed, waiting for you on arrival.

Recommendations

Merlot Vin de Pays D'Oc
Bellefontaine 2001 £1.99
Spicy, plummy and herby.

Rosé de Syrah Vin de Pays
D'Oc Bellefontaine 2001
£1.99
Juicy currant fruit.

Chardonnay Vin de Pays
D'Oc Bellefontaine 2001
£2.49
Tropical flavours, full bodied
and easy to drink.

Oxford Landing Chardonnay
2001 £2.99
A vibrant, rich, well made
wine with ripe melons on the
palate.

Bourgogne Blanc Chardonnay
Vaucher 2000 £3.29
A crisp, appley Chardonnay.

Jacobs Creek Shiraz
Cabernet 2000 £3.99
Ripe, juicy and a little spicy.

Chablis Vaucher 2001 £4.59
Lots of apples, high acidity
medium bodied Chablis.

P&O Ferries
On board

Map Ref: G1
Bus No:
English: Yes
Tasting: Promotion wines only
Payment: £, 💳💳
Parking: Yes
Open: Daily

P&O Ferries have a range of reliable wines, generally promoted with a buy 5 for 6 or 3 for 2 offers. Regard the prices shown here as a guide since their promotions change regularly. Beers can be good value especially when on promotion.

Other good buys on board are for smokers, rolling tobacco and cigarettes are generally half the price of those in the UK and sometimes even more.

Recommendations

Lamura Nero d'Avola Sicily £1.75
Round and warm, with extra smoothness. Plenty of flavour and good value.

Caneletto Pinot Grigio Garganega Veneto Casa Girelli £1.99
This is a simple dry non-offensive, easy to drink white wine. Ideal for parties.

Oxford Landing Sauvignon Blanc 2002 £2.50
Good, crisp, dry white, which is always consistent from vintage to vintage. You won't go wrong with this one. Good value.

Baron Philippe de Rothschild Chardonnay Vin de Pays D'Oc 2001. £3.16
This Chardonnay is a decent enough example.

Baron Philippe de Rothschild Cabernet Sauvignon Vin de Pays D'Oc 2000. £3.16
Decently gluggable bottle of wine.

Mumm Cordon Rouge Champagne. £12.30
Mumm is always a favourite and this bottle of bubbly is available at a decent price.

Auchan Hypermarket
Route de Boulogne (RN1)
Calais
Tel: 00 33 (0) 321 46 92 92
www.auchancalais.com

Map Ref: B5
Bus No: 5
English: Yes
Tasting: Promotional wines
Payments: £, 💳 💳
Parking: Yes
Open: Mon- Sat- 08.30-21.00
Closed: Sunday

Auchan Hypermarket has recently undergone a face-lift and is looking decidedly modern in its new domed roof. Inside it is bright, colourful and spacious.

The vast range of wines come predominantly from major French regions with a nod from Portugal, Morocco and Spain. Though there are some fine French wines on the shelves, wines tend to be mainly at the lower end of the price range. You can even buy cartons of wine from 40p, such as Ribaudour; don't sniff at this price, they are ideal for cooking.

How to Get There

From the ferry terminal take the motorway following the signs for Boulogne and exit at Junction (sortie) 14; just follow signs for Coquelles or Auchan.

From Eurotunnel cross the roundabout following signs for Calais and then follow signs for Coquelles or Auchan.

Foot passengers should take the free bus to the railway station and from here pick up bus number 5 which stops outside Auchan.

Sparkling wines are mostly French too. The range of champagnes and beers from around the world, are generally good value.

Don't forget the other products available at the hypermarket at up to 30% less in France. Refer to the 'Other Shopping Ideas' for examples.

Recommendations

Cellier des Dauphins Côtes du Rhône £1.49
This red gives off strawberry scented fruit and offers light, fruity, easy drinking. Hard to fault at the price, and it seems many shoppers agree

Touraine Sauvignon 2001 £1.60
This is a lightly scented white wine tasting of sherbet and apples. It has plenty of zest and needs a nice sunny day.

Chemin des Papes Côtes du Rhône 2001 £1.88
Simple, but gutsy enough at the price.

Château Suzanne Cahors 2000 £2.80
Deep, youthful colour. Fine aromas of tar and tobacco, good Cahors typicity. Dry, but full flavoured, attractive savoury side to it. Very classy at the price.

Clairette de Die £3.15
Fun fizz offering appealing floral aromas and soft, off-dry, grapey flavours. It's a winner at this price.

Chateau Loustalot 1999 Loupiac £3.76
Aromas of stone fruits and almonds. Good pure fruit on palate, very clean. Medium sweet, very crisp, refreshing.

Jacobs Creek Chadonnay Pinot Noir Brut Sparkling wine £4.74
For those who find Champagne too dry and a bit tart, this will probably work wonders – full flavoured and smooth bottle of fizz.

Pouilly Fumé Domaine des Mariniers 2001 £5.66
Pungent, nettley aromas, very expressive sauvignon. Lovely zesty example of Pouilly Fumé, reasonably priced.

Veuve Emille Champagne £7.08
Satisfyingly fruity at the price, and would suit those with a sweet tooth.

Carrefour Hypermarket
Cité Europe
Coquelles
Tel: 00 33 (0)321 46 75 55

Map Ref: A7
Bus No: 7
English: Yes
Tasting: Yes at the bar
Payment: £, 💳 💳
Parking: Yes
Open: Mon-Fri 09.00-22.00
Saturday 08.30-22.00
Closed: Sunday

Carrefour hypermarket is a giant, dominating the mouth of Cité Europe shopping complex. It stocks everything and anything at competitive prices. It is so huge that staff have to get around on roller skates!

Wines come from all areas of France and a smaller range is available from the rest of the world. There's also wines in 25cl cartons. A pack of 3 costs around 95p and are ideal for use in cooking.

Spirits are available in

How to Get There

From the ferry terminal take the A26 motorway following the signs for Dunkerque onto A16. Exit at Junction (sortie) 18; follow signs for Boulogne. Exit at junction (sortie) 12 sign-posted Cité Europe Ouest. Follow signs to Cité de la Europe, Centre Commercial.

From Eurotunnel cross the roundabout following signs to Cité Europe.

Carrefour is located on the ground floor.

---

abundance and the beers include a variety of continental beers alongside the ever popular Belgian beers.

Carrefour is an ideal shop stop and stocks a multitude of bargains. Check out the 'Other Shopping Ideas' section for more information.

Recommendations

Corbières 1998 £2.07
Soft, ripe, scented aromas with a pleasing mixed palate of brambly fruit and spice. Great for everyday drinking.

Carrefour Hypermarket

Tavel Domaine Amido 2001 £3.35
Remarkably gutsy for a Rosé. Demands cold meats, and would probably support a steak.

Crémant De Bourgogne Sparkling Wine £4.24
Crispy and fun.

Medoc Château Les Graves 1999 £4.34
This Cabernet Sauvignon offers a great mix of fruit and cedar tones. A well rounded glug and reasonable value.

Château Sainte Roseline Cru Classé 2001 Rosé £7.44
Pretty classy rose, delicate and lightly scented. Pure fruit on the palate, yet just off dry. Delicious.

Champagne Cheurlin-Dangin Brut £10.43
Very attractive Champagne. Plenty of flavour and nicely balanced, dry enough to refresh.

Meursault Laboure-Roi 2000
A classic Burgundy white offering nutty aromas and a attractive texture on palate with a fairly persistent flavour. Hints of New World style production. Good value at this price.

Champagne Veuve Clicquot Ponsardin £14.34
A richly flavoured, and with the finesse expected of this fine Champagne house. A reliable bottle of fizz.

Pierre Fournier, Carrefour's Manager, at the tasting wine bar

Bar A Vins

52 Place D'Armes
62100 Calais
Tel: 00 33 (0)321 96 96 31

Map Ref:	D3
Bus No:	7
English:	Yes
Tasting:	On request
Payment:	£, 💳 💿
Parking:	Around the square
Open:	Mon-Sat 09.00-19.00
	Sun 09.30-15.00
Closed:	Wednesday

Is there anyone in Calais more enthusiastic about selling quality French wines than Luc Gille? Luc and his wife Isabel are the team that make this petite, wine shop so adorable. Luc bubbles with passion as he enthuses about the wines he has personally selected at the vineyard. He has spent 15 years in the business so you can be confident of meaningful advice.

Recommendations

Sauvignon Touraine Vignoble Dubreuil 2001 £2.91
A fresh and balanced white number, easy to drink and good value.

Muscat Sec du Domaine Deshenrys 2000 £3.41
A floral nose with dry yet sweet flavours.

How To Get There

From the port turn right. At the second roundabout take the third exit (left) towards centre ville. At the end turn right into rue Molien. At the roundabout (Town Hall on left) turn right. At the traffic lights turn right into Place D'Armes. Bar A Vins is located at the opposite side of the square.

Château de L'Escarelle Coteaux Varois 1999 £3.53
Ripe, warm fruit, packed with flavour – great everyday drinking and great value.

Domaine Sol-Payre Cotes du Roussillon 2000 £5.05
An oaky, musty deep Southern French example with soft tanins and prune flavours.

Menetou-Salon Domaine de Loye 2001 £5.76
Crunchingly acidic white with greengauge fruit. Buy it if you dare.

Calais Vins

Calais Vins
Rue Gutemberg
Zone Curie, Calais
Tel: 00 33 (0)321 36 40 40

Map Ref: E6
Bus No:
English: Yes
Tasting: On request
Payment: £, 💳 💳
Parking: Yes
Open: Mon-Sat 09.00-19.00
Sun 10.00-17.00

JOINT BEST WINE TASTING FACILITY

A newcomer to Calais, Calais Vins specialise in French wines from various regions, some top notch, some easy drinking, and have created a convivial environment to welcome potential clients. An impressive feature is the fabulous temperature controlled tasting bar where you can taste around 22 wines at their correct temperature.

Just in front of their building they are cultivating their own

How To Get There

From the port turn left onto the motorway A16-A26 and exit at junction 15 (Calais St. Pierre). Turn right at the first round about.

vineyard. Perhaps Calais will become a wine making region.

Recommendations

Muscadet Sèvre et Maine Sur Lie 2001, Domaine Logis du Moulin £2.18
Fine, crisp, dry white, excellent example of Muscadet, would be lovely with light fish dishes or just light refreshment on a sunny day.

Château Lamour Saint-Emillion Grand Cru 2000 £8.13
Fine, plush St Emillion with good Merlot character which will stay at its peak for another year or two.

Chablis Premier Cru Fourchaume 2000 £9.00
A classic minerally, fruity Chablis, which will still improve.Reasonably priced.

Special Offer
Show your guide at the check out and receive a **free** membership card to the 'Calais Vins Wine Club' (worth £5) and instantly get **5%** discount on still wines.

Le Chais

40 Rue de Phalsbourg,
62100 Calais
Tel: 00 33(0)321 97 88 57

Map Ref: G4
Bus No: 2
English: A little
Tasting: Some
Payment: £, 💳 💳
Parking: Yes
Open: 09.00-19.00 daily
Closed: 12.00-14.00 daily

Le Chais has been a purveyor of fine French wine since 1865 earning it the accolade of being the oldest and most established wine merchant in Calais. The selection in-store, as always, provides an attractive range of tongue tickling wines.

Recommendations

Marcel Martin Touraine Sauvignon La Sablette 2001 £1.90
A dry white from one of the Loire's best producers offering attractive Sauvignon character and good value.

Les Hauts de Chaumet-Lagrange Gaillac 2000 £2.05
An easy drinking glug of baked fruit and ripe pruney flavours. Great value.

How To Get There

On exiting the port turn right following the sign to Centre Ville. At the roundabout take the second exit. At the end of the road turn left into rue Mollien. At the traffic lights turn right. Continue for 100 yards. Le Chais is on the right within an inlet.

Château Croze de Pys Cahors 1998 £3.98
A lovely mature red wine, aromas of walnuts and dried fruits. Lots of flavour, a dry finish. Best with food.

Les Genets Chusclan Côtes du Rhône Villages 2000 £4.25
Lots of juicy fruit and spicy tones - almost New World.

Château Lapiey Haut Medoc Bordeaux 1998 £4.65
A dry, mature claret, plenty of flavour. Drink with food. Good value.

Cheers

ZI du Beau Marais
199 rue Marcel Doret
Tel: 00 33 (0)321 19 77 00

Map Ref: 4J
Bus No: -
English: Yes
Tasting: Some
Payment: £, 💳 💳
Parking: Yes
Open: 24/7

How To Get There

Leave the port, turn left onto A26 motorway, take the first exit No. 3 to ZA Marcel Doret. Follow the sign ZI Marcel Doret on the roundabout below the auto-route. After Metro turn left at the roundabout. Cheers is next to the AA compound. Look for the big barrel.

Next time you visit Calais, look out for the barrel, because this huge barrel is actually the gateway into what seems like acres of wines, beers and spirits (1700 sq.metres to be exact) in all price ranges. And the last twelve months has seen Cheers expand two-fold to make space for a bigger range to include a variety of other products - such as mustard, Belgian chocolates and washing powder - generally known to be cheaper in France - so you can really roll out the barrel!

Recommendations

Beaujolais 2000 £1.60
A basic but very drinkable wine at this price.

Bordeaux Clossman Moelleux 2001 £1.99
Got a sweet tooth? this one is for you.

Michel Laroche Grenache 2000 £2.40
A warming, fruity but dry Southern French red.

Raymond Morin Domaine du Landreau Cabernet D'anjou 2001 £2.75
Sweet redcurrant fruit, with apple acidity. Chill it and drink it on a sunny day.

Domaine du Landreau Raymond Morin Coteaux du Layon 2001 (white)
Sweet, juicy, rich and fruity.

Montlouis Sec Domaine de Cray 1997 (white) £3.00
This is a lovely dry white from the Loire, beautifully crisp and dry.Michel

Laroche Merlot 2001 £3.05
Soft, fruity and very easy to drink.

Michel Laroche chardonnay 2001 £3.05
Pleasant on the palat and even a little smokey.

L'Heritage de Chantecaille 2001 £3.50
A well made, redcurrant fruit soft Bordeaux Rosé .

Chablis Raoul Clerget £4.20
A fresh, crispy highly drinkable Chablis.

Gigondas Louis Mousset 1998 £7.70
A pleasantly warming wine from Southern France.

FREE WINE

Spend £20 and get a **FREE** bottle of wine on presentation of this guide
The more you spend the better the quality of the free wine.

Only one per customer

Eastenders

14 rue Gustav Courbet,
Zone Marcel Doret
Tel: 00 33 (0)321 34 53 33

Map Ref: 4J
Bus No: -
English: Yes
Tasting: No
Payment: £, 💳 💳
Parking: Yes
Open: 24/7

How To Get There

From the Calais ferry turn left onto the A26 motorway and come off at the first junction junction (sortie) 3 following the sign to Z A Marcel Doret and continue to the roundabout

From Eurotunnel follow the A26 to Calais,, exit junction 18 to car ferry then exit 3. Right at roundabout, right at the next roundabout.

The Eastenders empire has been master-minded over the last decade by the infamous Dave 'ex-barrow boy' West.

The outlet is literally a massive warehouse - no frills here - just lots of wines. Alas, the charismatic Dave isn't to be seen much around here anymore, but a huge cut-out of him hangs on the back wall especially for those who miss him.

In the meantime, Marlene, Eastenders' wine buyer, has achieved an impressively mixed range from the 50p plonk to some fine wines. Beers are featured too with their own label ESP still doing well.

Recommendations

S Orsola Spumante £0.83
A sweet, grapey fizz.

Corbans White Label North Island Sauvignon Blanc Semillon 1999 £2.00
Lots of fruit packed into this price!

Côtes du Rhône Villages Jean Astier 2001 £2.00
Juicy easy drinking Rhône.

La Cave de Sigolsheim 1999 Riesling White £2.25
Off dry and fresh.

Crémant d'Alsace Brut Comte de Sigold Blanc de Blancs £3.25
A good fizz with crispiness and flavour.

ABSOLUTELY FREE!!

A bottle of Eastenders' own Lovely Bubbley sparkling wine for paying customers only on presentation of this guide

Only one per customer

Côtes du Rhône E. Guigal 2000 £4.00
A highly popular, easy drinking red wine.

Fleurie Maison Jean-Philippe Marchand 2000 £4.25
Lots of rhubarb flavours with some sweetness too.

Wolf Blas Cabnernet Sauvignon Yellow Label 2000 £4.95
Drinks like Ribena. Lovely.

Crozes-Hermitage E Guigal 1999 £5.50
Smokey and fruity character. Good Value.

Sauterns Chateau Placey, Michel Pascaud 2000 £6.75
Sweet, honey flavour with a touch of orange. Good value.

Cesari Amarone della Valpolicella 1997 £9.50
Raisins, sweet fruit, chewy.

Champagne Baron Fuente Rosé Delores £9.75
Salmon pink, dry and flavoursome. Good value.

Franglais Beer & Wine

CD 215, 62185
Frethun
Tel: 00 33 (0)321 85 29 39

Map Ref: Off the map at A7
Bus No: -
English: Yes
Tasting: Yes, extensive
Payment: £, 💳 💰
Parking: Yes
Open: Daily 09.00-19.00
Sat 09.00-18.30
Closed: Sun

Franglais' wine tasting facility is great. Olivier, the dynamic manager explained why he invested in the state-of-the-art wine dispenser: "All the wines in the Bar are individually stored at optimum temperature. This means the wine is tasted at its best." The range of 300 wines include the humble at 94p to Grand Crû Classé wines from Bordeaux and wines to lay down.

How To Get There

On exiting the port turn left onto A16-A26 motorway towards Paris-Reims. Continue to the autoroute to the A16 intersection. Take the A16 sign-posted Boulogne. Continue to exit (sortie) 11 sign-posted Gare TGV. Leave the autoroute and turn left over the bridge (D215). Franglais is 900 yards ahead on the right.

JOINT BEST WINE TASTING FACILITY

Recommendations

Château Maurine Bordeaux 1998 £3.49
Juicy, nicely balance, highly drinkable and great value!

Domaine des Salices Viognier Vieilles Vignes 2000 VDP D'Oc £3.51
Oaky on the nose followed by juicy, sweet flavours.

Crémant de Bourgogne Charles Roux 1999 £4.18
Tangy flavours with biscuity characters and a perfectly decent bottle of fizz especially at this price.

Intercaves

26 rue Mollien
62100 Calais
Tel: 00 33 (0)321 96 63 82

Map Ref:	E4
Bus No:	2
English:	Yes
Tasting:	Yes
Payment:	£,
Parking:	Outside
Open:	Tue - Sat 09.30-12.30
	14.30-19.30
	Sunday 09.30-12.30
Closed:	Monday and August

Intercaves, part of a nationwide chain, describe themselves as "Les Chevaliers du Vins" - the knights of wine! Wines are hand picked from individual growers and châteaux.

They lay claim to being leaders in vacuumed packed bag-in-the box wines You can taste any of the 25 varieties before you buy.

**EXCLUSIVE
SPECIAL OFFER:**
on presentation of the Channel Hopper's Guide A magnum of Côtes du Ventoux Rouge Cuvée Prestige when you spend £75 or more.

How To Get There

From the ferry terminal follow signs to Centre Ville (second exit off the roundabout) Continue straight on (railway on the right). At the end turn right into Rue Mollien. Inter caves is 200 yards along on the left hand side close to the traffic lights.

Oddbins

Unit 139, Cité de L'Europe
62901 Coquelles
Tel: 00 33 (0)321 82 07 32

Map Ref:	A7
Bus No:	7
English:	Yes
Tasting:	Some
Payment:	£, 💳 💳
Parking:	Yes
Open:	09.00-20.00 daily

BEST GLOBAL WINE MERCHANT

O ddbins have a petite, delightfully cosy outlet on the lower ground floor of Cité Europe and, perhaps, incongruously, opposite McDonalds. They have managed to cram in about 700 wines from all around the globe, at prices well below their UK branches. They are one of the few stores open on Sunday.

Recommendations

Bonassia Syrah £1.92
Warm, flavoursome, dry red example from Morroco. Good value too.

Côtes du Rhône L'Enclave des Papes £2.07
Decent, juicy Rhône red, sound everyday drinking.

How To Get There

From the ferry terminal turn left onto the A26 motorway. Follow signs to Dunkerque onto A16 motorway. Exit at Junction (sortie) 18 for Boulogne. Exit at Junction (sortie) 12. Follow signs to Cité de la Europe, Centre Commercial to Cité Europe.

From Eurotunnel cross the roundabout following signs to Cité Europe.

Oddbins is on the lower level.

Mirambelo 2000 £2.17
Good fruit, notes of walnuts. This Greek red number makes an interesting change.

Quiltro Merlot £2.36
This Chilean Merlot is full of soft, black fruits, highly flavoursome, easy drinking and great value.

Quiltro Chardonay £2.36
Nice, nutty Chilean character, pleasing touch of oak. Good depth and finish.

Virginie Syrah Vin de Pays D'Oc 2001 £2.78
Gutsy aromas, touch of sweet oak, lots of flavour, just off dry. Great Value.

Virginie Chardonnay Vin de Pays D'Oc 2001 £2.78
Excellent partner to the Syrah, this is really classy Chardonnay at the price, with plenty of flavour and well judged oak ageing.

Xerolithia Iieza Creta Olympias Dry White £2.87
Delicately scented, delightful wine, not too heavy, beautifully balanced, dry, crisp, refreshing drinking.

Yellow Tail Shiraz £3.21
Good juicy red fruit, plenty of flavour at the price!

Yellow Tail Chardonnay £3.21
Good, flavoursome Aussie Chardonnay, plenty to it.

Lingenfelder 2001 Riesling £3.21
Classy,tasty, Riesling. Long flavours, highly refreshing and great value.

Terra dei Messapi Brindisi Rosso 2000 £3.71
Fruit cake aromas,dry and flavoursome. Drink with Italian food.

Cosme Palacio Y Hermanos £4.24
Flavoursome Spanish white wine.

Chateau Maris 2000 £4.33
Top class wine from one of the most interesting estates in the Languedoc. Has warmth, spice and elegance

Ferngrove Vineyards Estate Chardonnay 2001 £4.33
Highly charged Ozzie Chardonnay with loads of flavour and oak. Lovely.

Porcupine Ridge Merlot £4.64 (South Africa)
A lovely merlot, sweet and juicy, chewy tannis. Good Value

Knappstein Riesling Clare Valley 2001 £4.95
Juicy, fresh fruit, lime, zest and lots of Oz character. Excellent value.

Wither Hills Sauvignon Blanc 2002 £5.76
Wonderfully zesty, easy drinking Kiwi Sauvignon -dry and refreshing and beautifully balanced.

Henri Harlin Champagne Brut £8.82
Great Champagne especially at this price. Dry and balanced.

Perardel
A Z Marcel Doret
62100 Calais
Tel: 00 33 (0)321 97 21 22

Map Ref: J3
Bus No: 1 (closest)
English: A little
Tasting: Yes
Payment: £, 💳 💿
Parking: Yes
Open: 08.30-19.45

How To Get There

Turn left out of Calais port onto the A26 motorway and exit at junction (sortie) 3. At the roundabout take the first exit sign-posted Zone Marcel Doret. Continue for a quarter of a mile until you see Perardel on the left hand side.

BEST WINE MERCHANT FOR THE DISCRIMINATING WINE LOVER

Perardel offers a pleasing mix of wines. In store, their top class range includes quality middle-range burgundies, clarets and white wines in £5.00-£10.00 price range.

Wines from Alsace and the Loire also feature to a lesser extent. Many French names and vintages are on offer such as Guigal, Chapoutier and there are many fine wines in the "sell the silver" price bracket such at Château Lafitte, Château Yquem, Petrus.

Perhaps unsurprisingly for an outlet whose head office is Reims there is an impressive range of champagnes including their in-house' Perardel' bubbly. In contrast there are some table wines which are sold en vrac (draught) from around 65p a litre plus a range of New World wines, and beers.

FREE WINE!

Spend at least £30 and receive a free bottle of quality wine.
The more you spend the better quality your free wine will be.
You must show your guide

Perardel

Recommendations

Prince des Gravieres Sauvignon 2001 £1.68
Good, sound dry white with pure sauvignon character. Excellent at the price.

Perardel Coteaux de Languedoc 2000 £2.47
Good everyday drinking and affordable at this price. Lovely warm fruit, and just a touch of the spice and scent so typical of the region.

Chardonnay Christian Adine Vin de Pays D'oc 2000 £2.57
Well made, fruity Chardonnay. Great Value.

Sauvignon de Bannay 2001 £3.27
Fresh, crisp and tart apples.

Domaine de Beauchene Costiere de Nimes 1999 £3.47
Robust southern fruity gutsy red. Good Value.

Petit Chablis Domaine Felix 2000 £4.45
Fresh and tarty just as it should be. Good value.

La Grand Moulin Premieres Cotes de Blaye £4.85
Made in the modern style with lots of coffee bean flavour. Good Value

Cremant de Loire Perardel £5.55
Fine bubbles. Good, dry earthy Loire character. Full flavoured and soft on the finish.

Châteauneuf du Pape Domaine du Vieux Lazaret 2000 £7.53
A powerful, sweet, fruity, wine. Great Value.

Chablis Premier Cru Montee de Tonnerre 1999 £8.21
Lots of character, minerally and fruity. Good Value

Volnay 1994 Domaine Carre-Courbin £8.42
A reasonable wine at the price.

Pidou
190 rue Marcel Dassault,
Zone Marcel Doret
62100 Calais
Tel: 00 33 (0)3 21 96 78 10

Map Ref: J4
Bus No: 1 (closest)
English: Yes
Tasting: Yes
Payment: £, 💳 💳
Parking: Yes
Open: 24 hours

Pidou have had the decorators in this year, and they look much better for it.

There are some attractive facilities on offer such as a spacious car park, coffee machines, currency exchange and even a special check-out for lorry drivers.

Shopping includes a souvenir shop, groceries and sandwiches. Outside there is a chippy and a hut selling Belgian chocolates. Inside there is a wide selection of mainly cheap French wines, but they do have a fine selection of beer to entice any passing trucker!

How To Get There

From the ferry terminal turn left onto the A26 motorway and exit at Junction (sortie) 3 following the sign to ZA Marcel Doret. Take the first left, you'll see a building called Alphanet, but a little further on is Pidou.

Recommendations

Baron de Saint Simiac Brut
£1.59
A basic fizz at a basic price.

Chablis Vignes Blanches
2001 £4.43
Mouthwateringly tarty.

Macon-Lugny Saint-Pierre
Bouchard 2001 £5.21
Fruity white and great value.

Sainsbury's

Sainsbury's

Route de Boulogne (RN1)
Calais
Tel: 00 33 (0)3 21 82 38 48
www.sainsburys.co.uk/calais

Map Ref: B5
Bus No: 5
English: Yes
Tasting: Yes
Payments: £,
Parking: Yes
Open: Monday to Saturday
08.30-21.00
Closed: Sunday

How To Get There

From the ferry terminal turn left onto the motorway and exit at junction (sortie) 14 following signs to Coquelles and Auchan Sainsburys

From Eurotunnel take the A16 motorway following signs for Calais exit (sortie) 14 then follow signs for Auchan Sainsburys

BEST VALUE CROSS-CHANNEL OFF-LICENCE

Sainbury's are located outside the Auchan commercial centre - handy if you want to do some grocery shopping at Auchan.

In general their products offer good value for money, especially their own branded products such as their Moscatel and superb value Brouilly. There are no rock bottom cheapies to be found, though. According to Sainsbury's wine buyer, Nico Thiriot, "There are many cheap wines in Calais, and there are as many bargain wines. Go for the bargain wines, then you can actually enjoy your wine and you won't wake up with a thumping head in the morning." We'll drink to that.

Inanda Brut Sparkling Wine
(South Africa) £2.37
Full of fruit and flavour,
good enough to drink on its
own or with orange juice.
Great Value.

Santa Julia Viognier
Mendoza 2002 £2.85
Good peachy fruit in this
Argentinian example.
Excellent at the price.

Sainsbury's Classic
Selection Muscadet Sèvre et
Main Sur Lie £2.85
A decent Muscadet and
good value at this price.

Sainsbury's Reserve
Selection Chilean Merlot
Colchagua Valley 2000
£3.32
Soft, fruity easy drinking –
very reliable.

Sincerely Sauvignon Blanc
(South Africa) 2001£4.95
Sometimes one hears that
Sauvignon smells of
asparagus, and here's a
good example. Dry,
scented, beautifully
balanced and very classy.

Barco Reale di Carmignano
Capezzana (Italy) £5.71
Really top class red at an
affordable price. Lots of
flavour and warmth and that
indefinable character that
makes good Italian reds go
so well with Italian food!

Reynolds Orange Moon
Shadow Chardonnay 2000
£6.67
For those who like their
Aussie Chardonnay rich and
full bodied, this is the one,
with plenty of oak to add to
the fruit.

Sainsbury's Extra Dry
Champagne £10.47
Sainsbury's own label
Champagne has always
been consistent and quality
is high. The fine, bready
aromas are typical of fine
Champagne, and the
flavours follow through well.

Duval-Leroy Brut
Champagne1996 £15.25
Really top class
Champagne, with plenty of
flavour and the overall
harmony typical of the very
best. Good now, but will be
even better if you can keep
it for 2 to 3 years.

Le Terroir
29 rue des Fontinettes
Calais
Tel: 00 33 (0)321 36 34 66

Map Ref: E5
Bus No: 16
English: Yes
Tasting: Yes
Payment: £,
Parking: Street
Open: Tues to Sat
          09.00-19.30
Sun   09.30-13.00

How To Get There

From the ferry terminal turn left onto the A16/A26 motorway and exit at exit (sortie) 15 junction sign-posted Calais St Pierre At the stop, turn right. At the roundabout take 3rd exit in the direction Calais Centre. Continue straight until the second roundabout and take first exit (right) following sign Calais Centre. Continue into rue de Valenciennes. At the end of the road turn left in front of the post-office. The shop is on the left side.

L e Terroir is a family-owned business run by the energetic Michel Morvan.

He has created a very pretty shop with a range of French wines starting at just £2. Le Terroir also sell complementary food items such as Terrins of Pâté, fois gras and snails and one of their specialities is making up baskets of their products beautifully wrapped for presenting as gifts.

The best part of the shop is located downstairs. As you descend you begin to detect a musty aroma and once on lower ground level you realise you are in an authentic wine cellar complete with dust. Some wines date back to 1876!

Recommendations

Château Nuit des Dames Côtes du Rhône £2.50 Reasonable value for a decent Rhône wine.

Grandin Methode Traditionelle Brut £3.25

Attractively priced for a sparkling wine of this quality, it has a touch of the biscuity character one associates with Champagne, and is dry and well balanced.

Pouilly Sur Loire Fouassier 2001 £3.65

Scented aromas of flowers and pears. Good, zesty flavours, nicely balanced dry white. A perfect everyday glug.

Michele Morvan in his wine cellar

Sancerre Le Clos de Bannon Fouassier £4.39

A lovely dry Sancerre, with good freshness and typicity. Extremely well priced.

Sancerre 2001 (Rose) £4.68

Good rosé wine is had to find -this one is a good find.

Chablis Premier Cru Cote de Lechet Gerard Tremblay 1999 £7.22

A top class Chablis. Tremendous verve and grip, this needs another 2 to 4 years to show at its best.

Tesco
Cité Europe, Coquelles
Tel: 00 33 (0) 321 460 278
www.Tesco-France.com

Map Ref: A7
Bus No: 7 Gare Calais Ville
English: Yes
Tasting: Yes, at the wine bar
Payment: £,
Parking: Yes
Open: Mon-Sat 8.30-22.00
Closed: Sunday

How To Get There

From the port turn left and continue onto the A26 motorway. Follow signs to Dunkerque onto the A16 motorway. Exit at Junction (sortie) 18 and follow signs to Boulogne. Exit at Junction (sortie) 12. Follow signs to Cité de la Europe, Centre Commercial. Tesco is on the lower level.

BEST CROSS-CHANNEL DRINKS SUPERMARKET

Tesco's bright drinks supermarket is situated on the lower level of Cité Europe. They offer over 650 different wines from 18 different countries and many are almost half the UK price. They also have a vast selection of beers and spirits making Tesco an excellent one-stop drinks shop.

Customers can benefit from the very British "car service" so you can shop 'till you drop and retrieve your purchases later from the collection point. This is a blessing leaving you to tour the rest of Cité Europe unburdened with heavy shopping.

Recommendations

Anjou Blanc £1.15
Lots of crispy apple tang.

J P Chenet Cabernet Syrah Vin de Pays D'Oc £1.45
This popular wine is both sweet and dry.

Valdivieso Cabernet Sauvignon (Chile) £1.72
Ripe blackcurrant juiciness. Good value

Cabernet de Saumur Rosé
£2.09
Redcurrent nose off-dry well made. Good Value

Muscadet Sevre et Maine Sur Lie Cos Noir 2001 £2.35
Fresh nose, spritz and bone dry fruit. Good value.

Proseco di Vldobbiandene D.O.C. Spumante La Gioisa £2.63
Sweet pear fruit and off dry. Good Value

Petit Bourgeois Sauvignon 2001£2.86
Grassy, crunchy with spearmint and gooseberry fruit. Great value.

Cremant D'Alsace Heimberger Brut £3.05
Fresh, crisp, slithgly sweet fizz. Good value

Domaine La Montagne D'or Seguret Côtes du Rhône Villages 2000 £3.75
Succulant and sweet. Very good value.

Côtes du Rhône E Guigal 2000 £3.76
Southern red, fruity and punchy. Good value

Tre Uve Ultima Italian Red £4.01
Sweet cassis flavour with a hint of vanilla. Good value.La Palmeria Merlot Rapel Chile 2000 £4.14
Big, intense, powerful and must be drunk with food. Good Value

Chapel Hill McLaren Vale Coonawarra Cabernet Sauvignon 1999 £6.89
Chocoholics will love this great value wine.

Sancerre Les Baronnes Henri Bourgeois 2000 £7.30
Pleasant sofe juicy red fruit flavours.

Tesco Champagne Premier Cru £9.17
An elegant bottle of fizz.

Wine & Beer World

rue de Judee
ZA Marcel Doret
62100 Calais
Tel: 00 33 (0)321 97 63 00
www.wineandbeer.co.uk

Map Ref: J4
Bus No: 1B (closest)
English: Yes
Tasting: Yes daily
Payment: £, 💳 💳
Parking: Yes
Open: 07.00-22.00 daily

Wine and Beer World are now owned by Majestic. They have turned a rather dowdy warehouse into a modern, well run drinks outlet.

The range of 650 wines starts at the 65p party wine right through to top-draw Clarets, including branded wines and Grande Marque Champagnes. Staff are bilingual and have been trained to give informed advice on the wines on offer.

Those who have shopped in Majestic in the UK may well wish to order in advance. You can do so on 01923 298297.

How To Get There

From Calais follow the A26 motorway link road to the first Junction (sortie) 3. Turn left, sign-posted Z.A Marcel Doret (Journey time around five minutes).

Recommendations

Cuvée de Richard Vin de Pays L'Aude 2001 (red)
£1.29
Fresh clean drinkable stuff. Good Value

Cuvée de Richard Vin de Pays L'Aude 2001 (white)
£1.29
Fresh, clean and drinkable. Good Value

Côtes du Rhône E. Guigal 1999 £4.49
Southern French warming style. Good Value

Château Grand Tuillac Cotes de Castillon 1999 Bordeaux
£4.99
Fruity but dry

Chablis Premier Cru Montmains Domaine Vocoret 1999 £8.49
Attractive minerally and intense flavours. Good Value

What is Cité Europe?

With representation from every European country, you instantly become an international shopper just by walking through the doors of Cité Europe!

Cité Europe is located in the village of Coquelles in Calais. Just a decade ago - prior to the development of Eurotunnel and Cité Europe - the area was simply a village road.

The name Coquelles is thought to be of Latin origin. deriving from the name of Eustache de Kalquella, who in 1183 was the first lord or Coquelles.

At that time the village, just a mere hamlet, was situated near the old tower remains of the 13th- century church of Old Coquelles.   Since then the area has had a series of European occupants: first the Romans, then the English for more than two centuries, the Spanish for a mere two years and the Germans for four years. How apt then that Cité Europe should be built on this very European site.

The philosophy behind Cité Europe is to bring to the shopper a truly cosmopolitan choice of shops. Each European country is represented in this immense indoor shopping centre.

Some 59,000 square metres on two levels is home to 11 major stores, including a hypermarket and 150 shops selling everything you can imagine from all over Europe.

Familiar names include **Body Shop**,

What is Cité Europe?

Etam, **Tie Rack**, **Toys R Us**, **Kokai** and **Naf Naf**. Stylish, casual wear is available at **Aigle** (highly regarded in France), **Zara**, **Carbonne and Jacqueline Riu**. For trendy kids clothes visit **Catimini** and **Petit Boy** and for shoes step into **Nikita K** and **Salamander**.

You may also want to dress your home. Whether you wish to add beauty with enchanting crystal, enhance your wine and dining experience with impressively designed porcelain and crockery and chic tablewear, a trip to **Geneviève Lethu** is recommended.

Electrical goods and cameras can be cheaper in France and **Darty** electrical store is a good choice. Find it on the upper level of Cité Europe.

What is Cité Europe?

Shopping is certainly the main event in Cité Europe, but it is essential to find somewhere to rest your weary feet and enjoy delicious food.

Head for the myriad of restaurants on the lower level. The dining area offers everything from sauerkraut to pizzas to hamburgers from the omnipresent McDonald's. There's even a pub where you can enjoy a pint or two.

Some parts of the dining area have been designed in the style of the respective country so as to enhance the international flavour and ambience.

Leisure is also considered an important aspect of Cité Europe. With this in mind Cité Europe also has a 12-screen cinema complex to accommodate all viewing preferences.

For the kids there is an adventure playground, a merry-go-round, simulators and a variety of video games.

And finally, not forgetting the wine, beers and spirits, you can enjoy a wonderful shopping day out and still go home with alcoholic bargains from Carrefour Hypermarket, Tesco Supermarket, Oddbins or Le Chais.

There is ample parking at Cité Europe car park. You can fill up with petrol at the petrol station located beneath the car park.

Opening hours:
Mon-Sat 8.30am-22.00

The centre is closed on Sunday.

How To Get There

Cité Europe is situated opposite Eurotunnel, ideal for those travelling with Eurotunnel.

From Calais port, turn left as you exit and join the A26 Autoroute. Then join the A16 Autoroute following signs to Boulogne exiting at Junction 12 (sortie 12).

Bus Route No: 7
Calais Map Ref: A7

Calais Restaurants

Aquar'aile
255 rue Jean Moulin
Plage de Calais
Tel: 00 33 (0)321 34 00 00
Fine seafood restaurant
on the 4th floor of a block
of seafront flats. You get a
fine view over the Channel
Tariff: £15-£50

La Bigoudène Crêperie
22 rue de la Paix, Calais
Crêpes
Tariff: From £6

Delices de la Ferme
Cité Europe, Coquelles
Tariff: From £5
Brasserie serving great
omelettes and pancakes.

Au Cote d'Argent
1 Digue Gaston Berthe
62100 Calais
Sea front restaurant with
panoromic views.
Quality fish restaurant
Tariff: From £10

Le Détroit
5 Boulevard de la
Résistance, Calais
Seafood, woodfire grills
Tariff: From £10

Le Milano
14 Place d'Armes, Calais
Pizzeria
Tariff: £8

Restaurant La Mer
30 rue de la Mer, Calais
Tel: 00 33 (0)321 96 17 72
A seafood restaurant open
12 noon to 12 midnight.
The menu includes
mussels, grilled fish and
meat dishes.
Tariff: from £6

Le Saint-Charles
47 Place d'Armes
(north side) Calais
Fish - monkfish in cider,
scallops - sirloin steak
Tariff: £7-£20

Le Sole Meunière
1 Boulevard de la
Résistance, Calais
Tel: 00 33 (0)3 21 34 42 30
Seafood restaurant also
serving steak grills
Tariff: From £10

Le Channel
3 Boulevard de la
Résistance, Calais
Tel: 00 33 (0)3 21 34 42 30
A gastronomic restaurant
offering a view of the port
and highly recommended
rustic style cuisine e.g.
sweetbreads and fish.
Tariff: From £10

★★★

* English Bar
* In the heart of the town
* The comfort of a grand hotel

43 Quai du Rhin
62100 Calais
Tel: 00 33 (0)3 21 97 54 00
www.metropolhotel.com

METROPOL'HOTEL

George V ***
36 rue Royale
Calais
Tel: 00 33 (0)3 21 97 68 00
Centrally located hotel.
Tariff: £35-£50

Holiday Inn Garden Court***
Boulevard des Alliés
62100 Calais
Tel: 00 33 (0)3 21 34 69 69
A modern, comfortable hotel.
Tariff: £55-£65

Formule 1 Hotel
Ave Charles de Gaulle
62231 Coquelles, Calais
Tel: 00 33 (0)3 21 82 67 00
A budget hotel offering value for money and easy access to the motorway.
Tariff: £20.00 approx for three people

Bellevue**
Place d'Armes
Calais
Tel: 00 33 (0)3 21 34 53 75
Located in Calais centre, close to the beach
Tariff: From £20.00

Metropole***
45 Quai du Rhin
Calais
Tel: 00 33 (0)3 21 97 54 00
www.metropolhotel.com
Tariff: £32-£40
A pleasant hotel with its own secure car park and mini British stylepub. The hotel offers very good value for money.
Special Offer:
Show your guide and receive a discount of 10% on the cost of your room.

Meurice***

5 rue Edmond Roche
Calais
Tel: 00 33 (0)3 21 34 57 03
www.hotel-meurice.fr
Tarrif: £34-£50

Located behind the fine arts museum and park Richelieu, this hotel is undoubtedly **the best three star hotel in Calais**. Its decor is very grand and elegant, adorned with antiques and fine furniture. The rooms are spacious and offer a variety of modern conveniences. Meurice even has its own gastronomic restaurant, La Diligence, and secure car park.

Copthorne***

Ave Charles de Gaulle
62231 Coquelles
Calais
Tel: 00 33 (0)3 21 46 60 60
A modern hotel conveniently located close to the Eurotunnel terminal and Cité Europe. It has its own swimming pool and gym and seems a favourite among the business community.
Tariff:£58-£68

D940 - The Scenic Route

D940, N1, A16 are the three different routes from Calais to Boulogne. Which do you take?

Once, the N1 was considered the main link between Calais and Boulogne. This was superseded by the A16-motorway, enabling a 20 minute dash between the two towns. Parallel to the A16 and N1 is one of the area's best kept secrets - the D940.

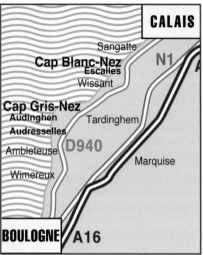

This is the scenic coastal route or Corniche de la Côte d'Opale which ambles lazily along the Côte d'Opale. It will get you to Boulogne... eventually. Head towards the harbour and pick it up by the Calais plage (beach) sign-posted Boulogne par la Côte and head in the direction of Sangatte. This long and winding road takes you through Blériot Plage which has its own claim to fame. It was here in 1909 that the famous aviator, Louis Blériot made his epic first flight across the Channel.

The road passes the eight kilometres of sandy beach and over to the undulating chalk hills of the twin headlands, Cap Blanc Nez and Cap Gris Nez where swimmers taking on the Channel come ashore. Take time out here and make your way to their tops for a great visual rhapsody of untamed cliffs, the rugged greenery and the blue of the sky all reflected in the expanse of the sea.

The land at Cap Gris Nez protrudes further out into the Channel, making it the closest point to the British Isles. It is also an ideal point for bird watching.

Sandwiched between these headlands are the tiny fishing villages of Escalles and Wissant.

In Escalles there's a fabulous, panoramic dining opportunity at a family run restaurant called Le Thomé de Gamond perched humbly on the top of Mont Hubert. The restaurant is designed so that diners are always assured a table by the window.

Next door is the Musée de Transmanche, a museum about the various historical attempts to cross the Channel either by air, sea, tunnel or by those who chose to swim! (Open daily from April to September - 10.00-18.00 - closed on Mondays. Entrance fee is around £2.00).

Wissant, a small seaside resort, has been nicknamed by the French as la **Perle Sauvage d'Opale**, the wild pearl of the Opal Coast. Perhaps this is due to its croissant-shaped stretch of white sand. It is also where the fisherman park their boats. You can sometimes see fishermen selling their wares almost straight from the sea. Their fishing boats containing the catch of the day are hauled into the village square and they trade direct from them.

Further along the coast the beautiful fishing village of Audresselles is home to a Hôtel de la Plage, a quaint restaurant. Audresselles still has its old Atlantic Wall fortifications dating from the German occupation. The fisherman here park their flobarts - fishing boats - by their homes alongside their tractors. The flobarts are blessed every year on 15th August - a ceremony carried out in period costume.

D940 - The Scenic Route

Dotted all along the D940 route are many temptations to lure you to stop and shop. You may see farmers selling their freshly grown fruit and vegetables in open huts. These are usually located by the roadside. Or you may see signs directing you to places where you can buy fresh seafood or flowers.

Further along are the quaint villages of Ambleteuse and Audinghen. Both villages are culturally noteworthy as each has its own war museum both of which are worth visting before moving on.

Audinghen is home to a quaint restaurant called L'Estival, housed in a wooden chalet and offers a convivial atmosphere.

The port at Ambleteuse was built by Vauban, the famous French military engineer. Its museum displays about 100 wartime uniforms.Situated at the foot of Boulogne, just six miles away, is Wimereux - a beautiful picture postcard seaside resort. Its sandy beaches make Wimereux popular with the French and tourists alike. During the summer the resort is buzzing with families and sunshine seekers.

As well as the promenade and the fine beaches there are pretty streets, winding roads and quaint cafés, restaurants and shops.

A few sand dunes later, the D940 finally ends and Boulogne begins......

Le Thomé de Gamond
Mont Hubert
Escalles
Tel: 00 33 (0)321 82 32 03
Tariff: From £10
Perched on a mountain top, this seafood restaurant offers a most agreeable environment in which to spend an afternoon. Each table has a window with a view over the countryside. Food can be variable though and we have received mixed reviews.

Restaurant du Cap
Place de la Mairie
Escalles
Cap Blanc-Nez
A particularly good seafood restaurant offering a provincial, French atmosphere in which to dine.
Tariff: From £9

L'Epicure
1 rue de la Gare
Wimereux
Tel: 00 33 (0)321 83 21 83
Seafood restaurant
Tariff: £13

Hôtel de la Plage
Bar and restaurant
21 rue Gustave Danquin
62164 Audresselles
Audresselles is a fishing village located off the D940
Seafood
Tariff: from £9.50

Les Dunes
48 Route National
Bleriot-Plage
Tel: 00 33 (0) 321 34 54 30
This is the first region leaving Calais onthe D940.
Tariff: £10.00 approx

Le Relais de la Brocante
2 rue de Ledinghem
Wimille
Tel: 00 33 (0)321 83 19 31
Situated in the village close to the church.
The menu includes kipper toast flavoured with coffee beans & tripe sausage with juniper.
Tariff: From £8

L'Estival
62179 Audinghen
off the D940 coastal road
Seafood restaurant
Tariff: From £5

Boulogne Town

Legend has it that in 636 AD a boat carrying only a statue of the Virgin Mary washed up on the beach of Boulogne and made it a pilgrimage site. Now they gather for the fish !

Boulogne has always been considered a very pleasant stopover, but those staying a little longer can enjoy the beauty, charm and heritage of both the old and new town.

The town itself is laced with quaint streets and shops and if you walk past the tidal harbour as far as the beach to the Sailor's Calvary you will be rewarded with a lovely view of the port.

If you venture higher up to the old city (vieille ville) you will find the appealing 13th-century ramparts - miraculously unscathed after World War II. They surround a network of narrow cobbled streets where you can find peace from the madding crowds and enjoy a peaceful and romantic walk.

The most vibrant street of the old town is rue de Lille, a cobbled pedestrianised road full of shops, restaurants and wine bars..Boulogne's claim to fame is that it is France's premier fishing port - in fact, a quarter of Boulogne's population are involved in fishing. A staggering 60,000 tonnes of fish are auctioned annually, making this the biggest auction in France. Moreover, every year Boulogne celebrates its Fête du Poisson (Fish Festival) during July when 20,000 fish and seafood enthusiasts come to enjoy the grand procession led in spirit by the Virign Mary in her capacity as patron saint of fishermen.

A major attraction is the Nausicaa national sea centre. It is only a few moments from the port with its own restaurant and multi-media library. At Nausicaa you can enjoy the maginificent wonders of the underwater world and experience the interactive terminals to the underwater observation tanks including the shark aquarium. To appreciate the aquatic education available, you should allow two fascinating hours. In case all that marine watching makes you hungry, Nausicaa also has two restaurants offering anything from a sandwich to a 3 course meal.

Boulogne has its own nature reserve at the Parc Naturel Regional Boulonnais. The area from the bay of Authie to the Oye beach, some 100km of coastline, is adorned with cliffs, dunes and marshes, and is preserved as a safe haven for birds and plants. Footpaths have been created for visitors and guided tours are organised to discover the national heritage.

Boulogne also has its own forest spanning more than 200 hectares. You can enjoy a ramble through the 13 kilometres of sign-posted footpaths or if you prefer more exhilaration, try cross-country horse riding. Alternatively you can hire a bicycle for a leisurely pedal through the countryside. Golfers can tee off at no fewer than three 18-hole golf courses: one at Wimereux and two in Hardelot.

Perhaps a little shopping at one of the hypermarkets or street markets followed by a drink and croissant, is more your style. If so, you will be pleased with the myriad of restaurants and continental style cafés Boulogne has to offer.

How to Get
From the Port to the Town

Turn right after customs, then right again after the Jean-Baptiste Pierre building, to the traffic lights and turn left. Pass under the flyover, turn left into the slip road to the traffic lights. The seafront is over the bridge - Pont de L'Entente Cordial - and then left. For Boulogne centre cross over the bridge to the Grande Rue - high street.

Nausicaa Centre National de la Mer
Bvd Sainte-Beuve Open daily - 10am-6pm. Tel: 03 21 30 99 99

Parc naturel régional du Boulonnais Maison du Parc à le Wast Tel: 03 21 83 38 79

Golf - (all 18 holes)
Golf de Wimereux, route d'Ambleteuse, Wimereux
Tel: 03 21 32 43 20
Golf des Pins
avenue de Golf, Hardelot
Tel: 03 21 83 73 10
Golf des Dunes
avenue Edouard VII Hardelot
Tel: 03 21 91 90 90

Horse Riding Centre Équestre du Boulonnais
Tel: 03 21 83 32 38

Bicycle Hire
Youth Hotel, Rue Porte Gayole
Tel: 03 21 83 32 59

Fish Market
Quai Gambetta Mon. to Sat. mornings. Opp. SeaCat Port.

General Market Days
Place Dalton.
All day Wed & Sat

Tourist brochures applaud the charm and beauty of Boulogne. But with a history of more than 2000 years, Boulogne is not just a pretty face!

Hôtel de Ville, Place de la Résistance

The Town Hall, loated in the heart of the Upper Town has been altered six times since it was built in 1735 (you'll see this date inscribed on the cornice of the Town Hall. With its classical layout it is the only monument in the Old Town built in brick and stone. Sculpted beneath the roof are the arms of the town: on the eft the swan and on the right the three massive heraldic balls. These emblems are part of Boulogne's coat of arms and have been since the 11th century.

It houses oil portrait paintings and the Wedding Room contains wood carvings from Dutch Oak.
Entrance from the Palce Goderoy de Bouillon
Tel: 00 33 (0)321 87 80 80
Admission free
Open Mon-Sat 8am-6pm.

Le Belfroi

(attached to the Town Hall) The 12th-century belfry is the oldest monument in the Old Town. It was once

used as a dungeon and symbolises communal liberty. It is worth visiting if only for the breath-taking views of the port, the town and the sea. Access is from the ground floor of the Town Hall. Entrance is free.

Traditional Fishermans Museum

A tiny but very interesting museum located inside an authentic fisherman's house inside the former Fisherman's quarter. It tells fishman's tales about living conditions and life in general in Boulogne at the beginning of the 20th century.
Rue du Machicoulis, Boulogne Sur Mer. Tel: 00 33 (0)321 30 14 52

Basilique Notre-Dame,
Enc de l'Evêche

Built between 1827 and 1866 by the Abbé Haffreinge, this hybrid cathedral was collectively inspired by St Paul's Cathedral, St Peter's in Rome, the Panthéon and Les Invalides in Paris.

It is located on top of a 12th- century maze of crypts and its dome dominates Boulogne town. The massive structure rises to a height of 101m. Of note is the High Altar of the Princes of Torlonia - a masterpiece of the 19th century Italian Mosaic.

The Cathedral has a crypt known as the **Crypt of Notre Dame** and boasts the accolade of being the second largest in France.

It has 14 chambers containing vestiges of the 3rd-century Roman temple. The treasure chamber houses some bejewelled religious artefacts of gold

The cathedral dome dominates the town of Boulogne

and silver. Among these objects is the Reliquary of the Holy Blood in gold, silver and enamel. The crypt was also used to house the mortal remains of the Libertador.

Notre Dame Cathedral
Admission free. Entrance from the Rue de Lille
Open daily from 8am-12noon and 2pm-5pm

The Crypt of Notre-Dame
Admission charged. Entrance from the Rue de Lille from the left porch.
Open Tues-Sun from 2pm-5pm.

Château-Museé
rue de Bernet

There is so much to see in this medieval castle and its museum that you may well run out of time. The castle was originally built by the Count of Boulogne and his wife Mahaut and was the first castle ever to be built without a keep in the history of military architecture. Part of the moat has been refilled with water and the drawbridge has been restored.

You can walk through the vaults and underground passages of this listed building including the chapel and the baronial hall.Do not miss the magnificent gothic Salle Barbière (armoury) adjoining the old prison.

In the museum you can enjoy antique Grecian vases, Gallo-roman antiquities, Egyptian sarcophagi, Renaissance coins, Eskimo and Aleutian masks and many exhibits brought back from Oceania 100 years ago by the sailors of Boulogne.

Les Remparts

Did you know that Boulogne is a walled city? The 13th century fortifications surround the cobbled streets of the Haute Ville. Built by the Count of Boulogne, Philippe Hurepel, the son of King Phillippe Auguste on the foundations of a Gallo-Roman wall, it has seventeen turrents and four gates, which have hardly changed since ancient times. The gates give access to the pathway round the ramparts. The fortifications and the castle are the best preserved from that period. in Northern France. Take a peaceful stroll along the ramparts to enjoy the panoramic views of the town and its coastline.

Rue de Lille

The bustling rue de Lille has always been lined with inns, hostelries and taverns throughout the middle ages. Candle-makers sold their wares to pilgrims who came to make their devotions to Our Lady of Boulogne.

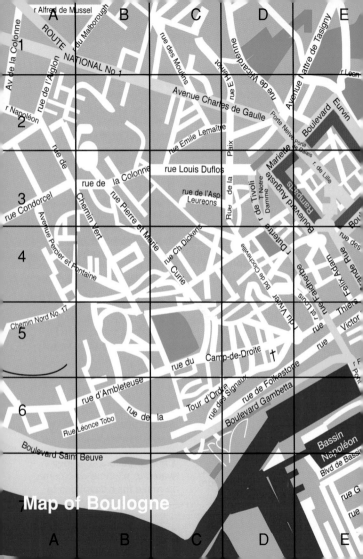

Map of Boulogne

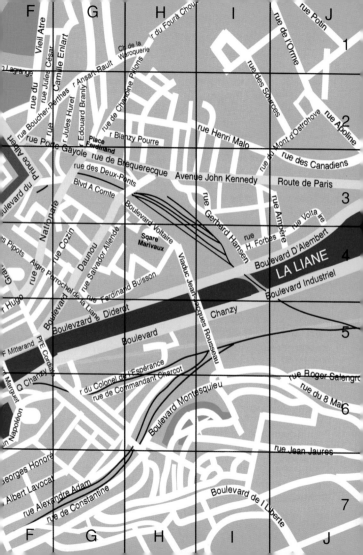

Auchan Hypermarket

Auchan
RN42
6220 St-Martin Boulogne

Map Ref:	Follow E1 direction
Bus No:	8
English:	No
Tasting:	No
Payment:	£, 💳 💰
Parking:	Yes
Open:	Mon- Sat 08.30-22.00
Closed:	Sunday

Auchan Hypermarket is considered to be the biggest and best place to visit in Boulogne for general shopping. It is brightly lit, spacious, and colourful.

How To Get There

From the port of Boulogne initially follow signs to St Omer and St Martin-B then signs for St Martin B-Centre. Follow the N42 straight through the town on the Route de St Omer and cross over the roundabout with McDonald's on the right. Cross over the next roundabout too, continue for 1.5 miles, take the exit Centre Commercial direct to Auchan and follow signs to Centre Commercial. Auchan will loom up ahead of you.

Cave Paul Herpe Wine Merchant

Cave Paul Herpe
85 rue Pasteur,
6220 St Martin Boulogne
Tel 00 33 (0)321 31 07 15

Map Ref:	Follow H5 direction
Bus No:	9
English:	Not much
Tasting:	En vrac
Payment:	£, 💳 💰
Parking:	Yes
Open:	09.00-19.00 daily
Closed:	for lunch & Sunday

This outlet specialises in the wines of the Languedoc. Buy the wine in bottles or on draught (en vrac). If you choose to buy en vrac, you can carry them

How To Get There

Take the A16 from Calais to Boulogne. Exit for the N42 signs to St. Omer and St. Martin-B. Follow the N42 through the town on the Route de St Omer. Turn left into Rue de la Colonne and 3rd right into rue Pasteur.

away in 10 or 20 litre cubis. Make sure you decant these within six weeks. Their best tipple is probably the Languedoc's most famous product. the sweet **Muscat de Riversaltes AOC**.

Boulogne Restaurants

Le Pot d'Etain
24 rue du Pot d'Etain
Boulogne
French cuisine
Tariff: From £5

Le Doyen
1 rue do Doyen
Boulogne
French cuisine served in a
candle-lit environment with
emphasis on fish dishes,
Tariff: From £9

Chez Jules
8 Place Dalton
Boulogne
Tel: 0033 (0)32131 54 12
A brasserie and a
restaurant so dine or snack
as you please.
Tariff: From £10

Cave du Fromager
23 and 30 rue de Lille
Boulogne
Tel: 00 33 (0)321 80 49 69
Situated in the cobbled old
town of Boulogne. Its
casual surroundings offer a
convivial atmosphere and
an imaginative menu of
cheese dishes.
Tariff: Average £7

Christophe et Laurence
10 rue Coquelin
Boulogne
Deli, steak, brasserie.
Tariff: £7.50

Irish Pub
6-10 rue Doyen
62200 Boulogne
Off Place Dalton

Estaminet du Château
2 rue du Château
Boulogne
French traditional cuisine.
Tariff: £8.50

Gourmandière
6 rue des Religieuses
(off rue Faidherbe).
Boulogne
Salads, omelettes, quiches,
traditional food.
Tariff: From £7

Le Matelote
80 Boulevard Ste-Beuve
Boulogne
Tel: 00 33 (0)321 30 17 97
Situated opposite the
casino.A gastronomic
restaurant specialising in
seafood. Good wine list.
Tariff: £15-£35

Formule 1
Z.I. de l'inquetrie
Rue Pierre Martin
St Martin les Boulogne
Tel: 00 33 (0)3 21 31 26 28
Tariff: £20 approx
No frills, but you do get a
TV and ensuite shower.

Hôtel Faidherbe
12 rue du Château
Boulogne
Tel: 00 33 (0) 3 21 31 60 93
Tariff: £45-£50

Au Sleeping*
18 boulevard Daunou
Boulogne
Tel: 00 33 (0) 3 21 80 62 79
Tariff: £19
A one star traditional family
run hotel.

Ibis Centre**
Boulevard Diderot
62200 Boulogne
Tel: 00 33 (0) 3 21 30 12 40
Tariff: From £37.00

Le Mirador**
2,4 rue de la Lampe
6220 Boulogne
Tel: 00 33 (0) 3 21 31 38 08
Tariff: £15-30

Paul et Virginie**
19 rue du Général de
Gaulle, Wimereux
Tel: 00 33 (0) 3 21 32 42 12
Tariff: £30.00
a cost hotel located just
outside Boulogne in the
seaside resort of
Wimereux.

Ibis Centre Vieille Ville***
Rue Porte Neuve
62200 Boulogne
Located close to the old
town and the ramparts.
Tel: 00 33 (0) 3 21 30 12 40
Tariff: From £37.00

Le Metropole***
51 rue Thiers, Boulogne
Tel: 00 33 (0) 3 21 31 54 30
Tariff: £35-£50

La Matelote***
70-78 Boulevard Sainte
Beuve
Boulogne
Tel: 00 33 (0) 3 21 30 33 33
Tariff: £30
This is a peaceful hotel
located on the sea front. It
has its own gastronomic
restaurant. Menus start at
around £15.

Dunkerque

It's Dunkirk in English, Dunkerque in French but both words are derived from the Flemish term - Dune Kerk - The Church of the Dunes

During the first millenium Dunkerque gradually developed from an inhospitable mass of silt washed over by raging seas from the Flemish coast into a thriving hamlet of fisherman. By natural design a series of dunes had formed consequently keeping the sea at bay and creating the lowlands.

The fishing community were of religious Christian persuasion and thus they built a church on the top of one of the dunes. In recognition of this, the town was named 'The Church of the Dunes' - Dunkirk/Dunkerque.

Being just a fishing port, Dunkerque was easily vanquished by the Spanish, French, English and Dutch. During the Battle of the Dunes in 1658 the Flemish Protestants gave Dunkerque over to Oliver Cromwell in exchange for the help of his Ironside troops in fighting off the Spanish. In 1662 Charles II sold Dunkerque back to the French for 5,000,000 livres, to be ruled by "Sun King" Louis XIV.

World War II brought mass destruction to Dunkerque. On 10th May, overwhelmed by the menacing German advance, Allied troops were driven back onto the beach at Dunkerque. The huge numbers of Allied troops were trapped and as they had nowhere else to go but into the sea they had become an easy target. So it was into the sea they went. "Operation Dynamo" called upon every available ship or boat to help evacuate 335,000 allied troops.

After five years of German

bombardment, Dunkerque was almost entirely demolished. Both the town and its economy had to be rebuilt. After a process of rapid commercial and industrial expansion, Dunkerque today is regarded as France's third largest port.

Though Dunkerque has remained in French hands ever since1662 the gastronomy available in restaurants, the festivals and flamboyant, colourfull street carnivals betray an innate Flemish culture and cuisine.

How to get to Dunkerque Town Centre

Dunkerque town centre is a full fifteen-minute drive from the ferry.

Take the A16 motorway in the direction of Ostend and exit at juncton 33 following signs to Dunkerque Centre. Turn left onto Avenue Rosendal which quickly turns into Boulevard St Barbe and follow signs to Centre Ville.

The Tourist Office
Le Belfroi
rue de l'Amiral Ronarc'h
59140 Dunkerque
Tel: 00 33 (0)3 28 66 79 21
Open: Mon-Sat
Closes 12.30-1.30 Mon-Fri

Following on from the above directions: Turn right after Jean Bart Square. You will see the belfry in front of the church.The tourist office is located inside the belfry.

Dunkerque

Who Is Jean Bart?

The townsfolk of Dunkerque are proud of the most celebrated corsair in French history - Jean Bart. He is a local hero whose memory transcends time by remaining firmly entrenched in the hearts of the people for more than three centuries, for he is the man who saved France from famine. His legacy is felt everywhere in the town and he certainly had the qualities of a hero. He started life as the son of an ordinary fishing and privateering family and though he rosethrough the ranks to the nobility, he maintained his straight talking and simple demeanour.
As a young man he joined the naval service under the Dutch Admiral Michiel de Ruyter. Nevertheless his allegiance remained with France and when war broke out between the French and Dutch (1672-78) he returned to Dunkerque to command a French fleet of small privateering vessels. In 6 battles he captured 81 ships. Louis XIV rewarded him by promoting him to Lieutenant Commander of the Royal Navy.

When wounded and taken prisoner by the English during the War of the Grand Alliance (1689-97) he escaped. He rowed from Plymouth for 52 days to the French coast. He made the English pay dearly for his treatment by capturing innumerable English ships.

His finest hour came in 1696 when his country faced famine. He set out with a Dutch squadron and captured 130 ships laden with Russian and Polish wheat, thereby saving the people of France from starvation. He was rewarded in 1694 when he was elevated to the ranks of the nobility with a peerage.

Three years later the Sun King Louis XIV personally announced a further appointment by saying: "Jean Bart, I have appointed you to the rank of Commodore." Not one to mince words, Jean Bart replied: "Sire, you were right to do so."

Jean Bart statue by David Angers (1848) on Place Jean-Bart

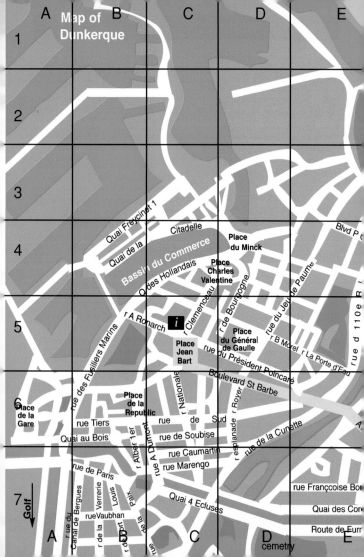

Auchan Hypermarket

Auchan Hypermarket
Route National 40
59760 Grande Synthe
Dunkerque
00 33 (0)328 58 55 55
www.auchan.fr

Map Ref: Follow G7
Bus No:
English: A little
Tasting: No
Payment: £, 💳 💳
Parking: Yes
Open: 8.30 to 20.30
Closed: Sunday

How to Get There
From the port continue straight on for 800 metres and take 4th exit at the roundabout (N1) direction Dunkerque-Port Est. 4km later it is on the right hand side of the Centre Commercial.
or Take A16 motorway, exit 25 sign-posted Centre Commercial, Grande Synthe.

Dunkerque has two hypermarkets, Auchan, the largest and Carrefour. Best buys are not only the wines (mainly French) beers and champagnes, but also mustard, olives, bicycles, garden furniture and baby car seats and accessories.

Carrefour Hypermarket

Carrefour Hypermarket
Saint Pol
59430 Saint Pol sur Mer
00 33 (0)328 58 58 58
www.carrefour.fr

Map Ref:
Bus No:
English: A little
Tasting: No
Payment:: 💳 💳
Parking: Yes
Open: 8.30-19.30
Closed: Sunday

How to Get There
From the port take A16 motorway. Exit at junction 29 and second exit off the roundabout, cross over the traffic lights, and next roundabout, then turn left at the second traffic lights turn left entering avenue de Petite Synthe (sign St Pol Sur Mer - Centre). At the second traffic lights turn right over a bridge towards Centre Commercial.

Bottles

Norfolkine Terminal
Dunkerque West Port
Tel: 00 33 (0)328 24 95 30

How to Get There
As you go to exit the port, Bottles is situated on the left hand side before you leave.

Map Ref:
Bus No:
English: Yes
Tasting: No
Payment:: 💳 💳
Parking: Yes
Open: Mon 08.30-18.00
Tues-Fri 09.00-21.00
Closed: Sunday

It's a small outlet but it does have all the big brands and probably the only outlet in Dunkerque that can supply a reasonable global range.

Recommendations

Hugh Ryman Merlot £1.45
A plummy little number and very good value.

Domaine de Cibadies Chardonnay 2001 £2.00
A simple but pleasing Chardonny, highly drinkable and offers good value.

Bourgogne Hautes Côtes de Nuits Pinor Noir 1999 £2.25
Lots and lots of strawberry fruit with lots of tannins to give body. Great value.

Gran Sangre de Toro Vendimias Selectas Torres 1999 £4.60
A ripe, crunchy, vibrant red with spicy fruit and lots of juicy flavours. Great value.

Chablis Michel Laroche 2001 £5.30
This is all a Chablis should be, great fruit combined with minerally tastes and smokey character. Great value.

Wolf Blass South Australia Chardonnay 2000 £5.85
Creamy and tropical yet off dry. Lovely.

Maxim's Champagne Brut £12.50
Lots of fruit in this fizz.

Cave Paul Herpe
208 rue de la République
Saint Pol Sur Mer
00 33 (0)328 60 99 19

Map Ref: J4
Bus No: -
English: A little
Tasting: En Vrac wines
Payment: £, 💳💳
Parking: Yes
Open: 09.00-19.30
           Sun 09.00-12.30
Closed: 12.30-14.30
           All day Monday

How to Get There
From the port take A16 motorway. Exit at junction 29 and firstt exit of the roundabout following sign to St Pol Sur Mer-Carnot. At the next roundabout take second exit (ie. straight across), left at the junction and continue straight over the traffic lights following signs to St Pol Sur Mer. At the next set of lights turn left following signs to Centre Ville into Rue de la République and continue for five minutes.

Cave Paul Herpe belongs to a chain of shops which specialise in the wines of the Languedoc region in Southern France.

At Cave Paul Herpe you have the choice of buying your wine the French way en vrac (draught), or in bottles. For a small charge you buy a 10L or 20L container called a cubi and fill it with any one of the wines available en vrac.

These start at a simple table wine for .93p per litre to a sweet Muscat de Riversaltes AOC, the wine the Languedoc is most famous for - at £4.20 a litre.

Dunkerque Restaurants

Bistrot de la Plage
24 Digue de Mer
Dunkerque Malo Les Bains
Tel: 00 33 (0)328 65 01 11
Tariff: from £9
Open: 11.30-14-30 and
18.30-22.00. Primarily a
seafood restaurant which
also serves regional
specialities and salads. The
restaurant has a sea view.

Le Grand Morien
Place Jean Bart
Dunkerque
Tel: 00 33 (0)328 66 55 18
Tariff: from £7
Open: 19.00-midnight
Brasserie style restaurant

Le Roie de la Moule
129 Digue de Mer
Dunkerque Malo les Bains
Tel: 00 33 (0)328 69 25 37
The name of the menu
means "King of the
Mussels' and describes the
menu well. There are 9
preparations of mussel
dishes and other seafood.
Tariff: Av. £10
Open: 19.00-midnight

McArthur
3 rue Belle Vue
Dunkerque
Tel: 00 33 (0)328 63 54 63
Tariff: various
Open: Mon-Fri 11.00-02.00
Sat 19.30-02.00.
A pub serving pub grub
French style at lunchtime.
Murphy's and Heineken are
sold. It is regarded as one
of the town's hot spots.

Les Trois Brasseurs
ZAC Des Bassins
Pôle Marine
Dunkerque
Tel: 00 33 (0)328 59 60 60
Tariff: various
A restaurant with its own
brewery serving typically
Flemish cooking. The
restaurant is decked out in
brewery style decor.

L'Art des Choix
451 rue Winston Churchill
Dunkerque
Tel: 00 33 (0)328 69 38 19
Tariff: £10
Regional French cuisine

Dunkerque Hotels

Hotel Borel*
6 rue l'Hermitte
Dunkerque
Tel: 00 33 (0)328 66 51 80
Comfortable 48 roomed
hotel located near the port
in the city centre.
Tariff: From £39

Hotel Welcome*
37 rue Poincaré
Dunkerque
Tel: 00 33 (0)328 59 20 70
Tariff: From £37

Europe Hotel*
13 rue du Leughenaer
Dunkerque
Tel: 00 33 (0)328 66 29 07
Central location. Rooms
have recently been
refurbished. The hotel has
its own seafood restaurant.
Tariff: From £37

L'Hirondelle*
46/48 Avenue Faidherbe
Dunkerque-Malo
Tel: 00 33 (0)328 63 17 65
This 48 roomed hotel is
conveniently located in the
heart of malo-Les Bains
close to the beach. It has
its own seafood restaurant.
Tariff: From £30

Hotel du Lac
(Best Western)
2 Bordure du Lac
Ambouts-Cappel
Dunkerque Nord
Tel: 00 33 (0)328 60 70 60
A comfortable chain hotel
with its own restaurant.
Tariff: From £30

Au Rivage*
7 rue de Flandre
Dunkerque
Tel: 00 33 (0)328 63 19 62
The hotel is located near
the seaside. It has its own
seafood restaurant.
Tariff: From £29

Trianon Hotel
20 rue de la Colline
Dunkerque
Tel: 00 33 (0)328 63 39 15
Tariff: From £26

Le Transat
3 rue de la Digue
Dunkerque Malo
Tel: 00 33 (0)328 63 50 05
Tariff: From £28
19 roomed hotel near the
beach with a swimming
pool, casino, bar and
restaurant.

There is only one word for

Le Touquet

....Style

You know you have entered Le Touquet when the road ahead changes colour as if laid out like a regal red carpet. It may seem a little pretentious but this is just the beginning of your journey into style.

Shoppers can relish the chic designer shops while sun worshippers can enjoy the fabulously clean and well maintained seafront and beach - either below the promenade or more discretely in the dunes. The sporty sort can sail, windsurf or even take instruction in sand yachting from none other than Bertrand Lambert - the world champion.

Equestrian enthusiasts should head for the shady beauty of the forest and indulge in horse jumping or racing at the Hippodrome. It is located within the grounds of the Parc International de la Canche where a well established

equestrian school is run. The centre also arranges romantic horse rides along the coast at dawn, and, when the night is clear, even in moonlight.

Tennis players can play on the outdoor or indoor courts (with natural light) where champions have played before.

Le Touquet has its own golf course which has the double accolade of being the international champion-ship course and considered the most beautiful in France.

Located on the seafront is a Thallasa health and relaxation centre where clients are pampered with concoctions containing oceanic minerals. Their health 'cures' are designed to rejuvenate, stimulate, invigorate or just relax.

Meanwhile the kids can enjoy a day at the Aqualud

water adventure park also on the seafront - a fabulous tropical themed indoor and outdoor swimming pool with flumes, water toboggans and other pool side rides.

Culture vultures need only stroll through the pristine streets and observe as the diverse architectural history unfolds. The buildings are a collage of several varieties of seaside styles from different eras. Although they are startlingly different from each other, they somehow blend well together.

How to get to Le Touquet

From Calais take the A16 motorway in the direction of Dunkerque. Follow motorway signs to Boulogne. Between Boulogne and Le Touquet there is a toll to pay. Exit at Junction (sortie 26) at Etaple, Le Touquet. Simply follow the signs. Journey time: 1 hour.

The differing styles have evolved because, amazingly, while Le Touquet's neighbouring coastal towns were destroyed by the wars, Le Touquet itself remained unscathed. Moreover, it was during the period between the two world wars that Le Touquet rose to the stature of chic in the eyes of the British holidaymakers.

The Past
The history of the town started in the hands of a notary called Alphonse Daloz. He bought the land in 1837 in the hope that it was arable. He planted an assortment of vegetables and cereals, pine and other attractive trees. Only the trees survived, but when they matured by the end of the century Le Touquet had become a most appealing forest by the sea.

Le Touquet's prosperity was sealed when In 1903 two Englishman, John Whitely and Allen Stoneham bought the forest (known then as la Fôret) and formed a company called Le Touquet Syndicat Ltd. The company built expensive villas and hotels and sold the villas to the rich and famous of London. The extensive advertising in the British media contributed much to the general awareness of Le Touquet.

Soon famous names such as PG Wodehouse and Noel Coward bought villas within the forest and the luxury hotels filled up with weekending English nobility.
By the 1920's it had become **the** place for the jet set to weekend. These days it is mostly the rich Parisiens who own the expensive villas in the forest. Some say it is like a little bit of Paris by the sea and this belief is reflected in the name Le Touquet Paris-Plage.

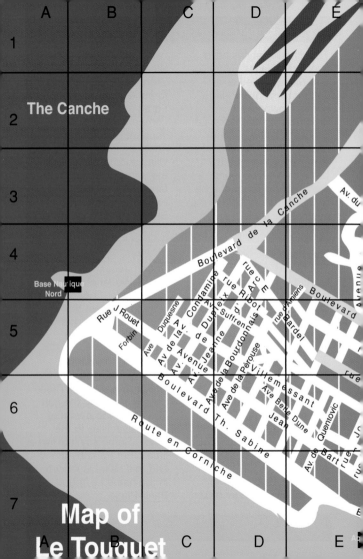

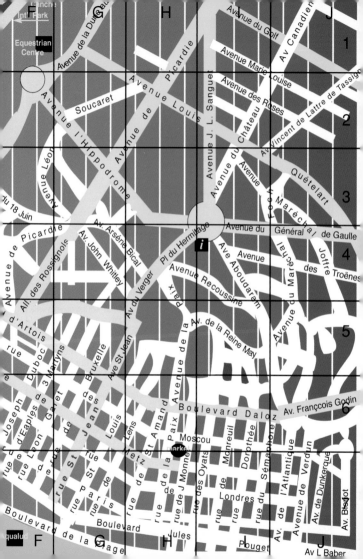

Le Touquet

Tourist Office
Palais de l'Europe
Place de l'Hermitage
Le Touquet
Tel 00 33 (0)321 06 72 00

Covered Market
rue Jean Monnet
Open daily from April

Race Course
Ave de la Dune aux Loups
Tel: 00 33 (0)321 05 15 25

Pony Rides
Hippodrome de la Canche
Tel: 00 33 (0)321 05 20 97

Sailing activities:

Base Nautique Nord
Cercle Nautique du Touquet
Tel: 00 33 (0)321 05 12 77

Bas Nautique Sud:

Speed-sailing
Hervé Spriet
Tel: 00 33 (0)1 42 88 09 43

Sand Yachting
Bertrand Lambert
Tel: 00 33 (0)321 05 33 51

Golf du Touquet
Avenue du Golf - BP41
Tel: 00 33 (0)321 06 28 00
Two 18-hole golf courses

Swimming
Aqualud - Parc Aquatic
Tel: 00 33 (0)3 21 05 63 59

Thalassotherapy
Sea front
Tel: 00 33 (0)321 09 86 00

Le Touquet Museum
Corner of Avenue du Golf
and Avenue du Château
Tel 00 33 (0)321 05 62 62

Tennis Club des 4 Saisons
Avenue de l'Hippodrome
Open daily 08.00-22.00rhrs
Tel: 00 33 (0)321 05 02 97

A Must See - Life at Sea

Just before Le Touquet you will pass through a fishing village called Etaples Sur Mer. Stop off here and visit the **Maréis Museum.** This new museum depicts the life of the local fishermen and their wives. There are several displays - some interactive, 3D films and a touch pool.

Maréis Museum
Centre de la Pêche
Artisanale, La Corderie
Boulevard Bigot-Descelers
62630 Etaples Sur Mer
Tel: 00 33 (0)321 09 04 00
www.pas-de-calais.com
Adults £4.50 Kids £3

A Tour Around The Shops -

Most of which are

branches of Paris shops

The best shopping is at **Rue St Jean**. The road stretches from the seafront to the Casino and the fabulous Westminster Hotel. Our tour starts at the seafront.

5 Nota Bene Pia
This shop specialies in stylish Aigle shoe wear. No self- respecting local would be seen on the beach promenade in anything less. It's a jet set thing.

7 Geko
Sells ethnic style products and jewellery including cowboy hats made of real cow hide. How chic!

9 Flais Gérard
Antique lovers would be impressed with this shop. It exudes style. Even before you enter, the extensive wood carvings decorating the exterior top to bottom create quite an impression.

Inside there is a mixture of French and other European antiquities that any antique officanado would be proud to display.

12 Comptoir des Isles
On the shelves is a curious mix of quality bric-à-brac

Rue St Jean

and some lovely - if a little frumpish - clothes.

14 Betty Bop
Betty Bop is full of pretty girly clothes with lots of flouncy frills.

16 Carat
An expensive jewellery shop but the designs are quite stunning.

21 Barque en Ciel
This is a play on the words "arc-en-ciel' - a rainbow. It is a lovely seaside shop selling sea shells and maritime toys. There are also some fantastic ships complete with sails, available in many sizes including miniatures.

33 Love Love
A bedtime shop for, it would seem, eccentric batchelors. Socks come with corny cartoon pictures to match boxer shorts and slippers. A set with teddy bears is particularly lovely.

35. Paris Voy
This is a lingerie shop for the modest woman however, there are some sexy stockings on display in the window.

36 Only Cool People
If you think your children are trendy, this is the place to shop for them.

37 Rien Que Pour Elles/Lui
Whoever your favourite designer is you are bound to find something of their collection at this chic outlet. Labels include Paul Smith, Moschino and Jean Paul Gaultier.

38 Les P'tits Branchés
More stylish clothes but for slightly older trendy teens.

40 Chez Martin
Looking good on the golf course or the tennis courts is essential fo serious players. Chez Martine are specialists in providing the winning kit.

42 Rodier
Rodier offer beautiful and stylish clothes for women.

43 Les Poteries du Logis
This quaint shop sells pretty pottery with a rustic feel.

7 Au Chat Bleu
Chocoholics will love Le Chat Bleu. It is famous throughout Le Touquet for its divine hand-made chocolates. The owners insist that they invented 'Le Bouchée' - literally a mouthful but actually a chcolate bar. Choose from 56 varieties.

48 Terrne et Ciel d'Opale
A quality gift shop selling dolls, books, trinkets and divinely scented soaps.

56-61 La Mascotte
La Mascotte is a series of shops located on both sides of Rue St Jean. It is a shopping centre for an endless range of quality goods and the shop the jet set choose to place their wedding lists. British tourists in the know come here to get their hands on Lalique crystal at one third off the UK price. Everyone else shops here for their leather bags, Cartier, Hermès, Baccarat and Christofle products. All in all this is a lovely place to browse.

Le Touquet Market
The semi-covered market is open every Saturday morning at **Rue de Metz**.

The town of Le Touquet is in itself a "Sight". Just walk around

Nestling between the sea and the forest, Le Touquet offers a range of sights. As the resort developed, different architects left their mark making the streets an exhibition of diverse architecture.

The area of **Le Village Suisse**, for instance, is tinged with medieval influences, whereas Villa le Castel in **rue Jean Monnet** shows off its neo-medieval style. **Avenue de la Reine Victoria** on the other hand has two adjoining buildings Villa Glenwood and Villa Karidja built with exceptional style in symmetry.

As in any French town Le Touquet's Town Hall in **rue des Oyats** represents a lovely architectural feature. It is made from local stone and flanked by an imposing belfry. Its chunky features are very 1920s anglo-Norman, resembling a lord's manor house.

To learn more about the endless architectural styles, visit Le Touquet Museum on **Avenue du Golf** for a good review of the architectural history. The museum itself is housed in a typically handsome 1930s Le Touquettois villa. Paintings by the noted landscape artist **Edouard Leveque** are on display within the museum. It was through his paintings that Leveque inadvertently gave the Opal Coast its name. His palette consisted mainly of pinks, beiges and slightly iridescent colours resembling the hues of opal stone.

Rue St Jean is probably the liveliest area especially around the beach, where you can walk on the promenade, bathe in the sun shine or the sea, or participate in beach sports.

On the sea front look out for the diving board. It may seem odd to include a diving board in a town's list of monumental heritage, but this is no ordinary diving board - it was the first diving board to appear in France. When built in 1948 by the architect Louis Quételard it was very futuristic structure and became synonymous with "le Style Touquettois Moderne". Anyone bold enough to use the board was regarded as fashionably avant garde - and if that someone was a woman in a bathing suit, even a tad risqué. Today it remains a symbol of modernity of post-war Le Touquet

Rue Jeanne Monnet leads to the arch of the covered market. Unlike other markets this moon-shaped monument,

decorated with off white tiles is a listed building. The beautiful, brick built, white-washed structure was the design of the architect Henry-Léon Bloch and built between 1927-1937. The market's covered area, adorned with attractive tiling, is where the perishable products such as cheese, meat, fish, fruit and vegetables are sold. The central courtyard is covered with stalls selling superb top quality textiles, clothes and shoes at market prices.

Apart from the colourful echoes of French life the market also offers two fine vistas: the sea and the Jardin d'Ypres.

The 1900 acre forest is very well-manicured. The trees include maritime pine, birch, alder, poplar and acacia which offer fine shelter from the wind for around 2000 Anglo-Norman and modern luxury villas.

Flavio
1 Ave de Verger
Le Touquet
Tel: 00 33 (0)321 05 10 22
Flavio offers gastronomic
and delicious cuisine in
gorgeous, elegant
surroundings.
Tariff: £23

Le Café des Arts
80 rue de Paris,
Le Touquet
Tel: 00 33 (0)321 05 21 55
The restaurant offers fine
nouvelle cuisine. The walls
are covered in works of art
which are for sale.
Tariff: £30

L'Escale
Aérodrome, Le Touquet
Tel: 00 33 (0)321 05 23 22
The large local clientele
confirms the restaurant's
quality cuisine.
Tariff: From £8

Le Nemo
Boulevard de la Mer
Le Touquet
Tel: 00 33 (0)321 06 20 66
Informal cuisine
Tariff: from £6
Submarine themed decor
serving a mix of traditional
and regional dishes.

Red Rock Café
69 rue de Paris
Le Touquet
An informal restaurant
Open to 4am

Les Sports
22 ru St Jean
Le Touquet
Tel: 00 33 (0)321 05 05 22
Tariff: £12
An informal quality
restaurant, open all day
serving steaks, and welch
rarebit. Regarded highly
locally.

Sogeto L'Escale
Avenue de Picardie
Le Touquet
Tel: 00 33 (0)321 05 23 22
Tariff: From £6.00
Friendly restaurant serving
both traditional and rgional
food.

Ibis**
Front de Mer, Le Touquet
Tel: 00 33 (0)321 09 87 00
Tariff: From £35
Conveniently attached to the Thalasso centre on the beach front.

Novotel Thalassa***
Front de Mer, Le Touquet
Tel: 00 33 (0)321 09 85 00
Tariff: From £60
Conveniently attached to the other side of the Thalasso centre on the beach front.

Park Plaza Hôtel ****
4 Boulevard de la Canche
Le Touquet Paris-Plage
Tel: 00 33 (0)321 06 88 88
Tariff: From £50
A beautiful hotel located in the forest. It offers a fabulous range of Thalgo beauty and relaxation treatments.

Holiday Inn Resort****
Avenue de Maréchal Foch
Le Touquet
Tel: 00 33 (0)321 06 85 85
Tariff: From £50
Everything you would expect from a 5 star Holiday Inn.

The Westminster ****
Avenue du Verger
Le Touquet
Tel: 00 33 (0)321 05 48 48
Tariff: From £50
The Westminster (shown below) is a magnificently luxurious hotel. It has a hall of fame of signed photos of the rich and famous.

Which French Wine?

France is one of the leading wine producing countries and this is reflected in the French outlets where most, if not all, of their selection is French. With so much choice, it helps to know a little about French wine.

First, inspect the label for an indication and therefore an assurance of the quality of the wine. The best wines of the regions have Appéllation Contrôlées on the label which gives a guarantee of the origin, supervision of production method, variety of grape and quantity produced.

Less controlled but still good value wines are listed as Vins Délimités de Qualité Supérieure (VDQS) and are worth trying. There are also the Vins de Pays. These are country wines, more widely found in the South of France, which do not specify the exact location of the vineyard but are generally worth a try and often offer the best value for money. Great examples are

Vin de Pays du Gard and the wines from Côtes de Gascogne. Further down the ladder are the Vins de Table. They are varied in quality but are so cheap that they are worth a gamble. You could be pleasantly surprised for as little at 60p-£1.50.

We have categorised the wine growing areas broadly into seven major regions. These are: Alsace, Burgundy, Bordeaux, Champagne, Loire, Midi and Rhône.

Alsace

The Alsace is situated in eastern France on the German border. The wine labels from this area differ from the rest of France by calling the wine by the name of the grape rather than the area e.g. Gewürztraminer, Riesling. A label with Alsace AC denotes the standard Alsace wine which is typically Germanic in character, often being aromatic and fruity, but drier than its German equivalent. A label with Alsace Grand Cru printed on it indicates a higher quality and only the four most highly regarded grape types can be used in its making and they are: Gewürztraminer, Riesling (not to be confused with the German wine of the same name), Tokay Pinot and Muscat. These are medium priced white wines with reliable quality and are generally dry to medium dry. The Alsatian wines are great aperitifs and also combine well with fish, poultry, salads or with a summer meal. Expect to pay: £1.66-£3.33 per bottle.

Which French Wine?

Bordeaux

Bordeaux is in the southwest region of France with the Dordogne region on its eastern border and the Atlantic Ocean on the west.

The term Claret refers to the red dry wines of this region and wines such as Médoc, St. Emillion and Pomerol which are in the lower price range.

There are also numerous wines known by the name of Château. Quality, especially at the lower end, can be variable. Claret goes well with meat, chicken and cheese.

Expect to pay: From as little as £1.55 per bottle, to more than £12.50 for a top class Château.

Situated between Bordeaux and the Dordogne valley is an area called Bergerac. Bergerac has a complete range of wines of its own; most commonly Bergerac (red, rosé and dry white), Côtes de Bergerac (red and medium sweet wine),

Monbazillac (sweet white) and Pécharmant (fine red).

Expect to pay: £1.10-£1.77 for the Bergerac. £3.33 for Monbazillac.

Burgundy

Burgundy is an area of France southeast of Paris running from Chablis at the northern end, down through to Lyon at the southern end. About 75% of the wine production in this region is red with the remainder white.

It is worth noting the area on the label when choosing a Burgundy wine since the more exact the area, the finer the wine is likely to be. The best are labelled "Grand Cru", followed by "Premier Cru", "Villages", a specified region and finally, the most basic will have just "Burgundy".

The best known of the whites is Chablis which is in

the higher price bracket. The Côte de Beaune produces some of the finest such as Meursault and some good light dry wines come from Mâconnais such as Mâcon Blanc and Pouilly Fuissé. All Burgundy white wines are dry and are an ideal accompaniment for fish.

The finest red Burgundy wine comes from the Côtes de Nuits such as Nuits St Georges and the Côtes de Beaune namely Pommard, Volnay and Monthélie. These are best drunk with meat, game and cheese.

Expect to pay: £3.80-£7.80 These wines tend to be reliable in this price point.

Best known of the reds in the south of this region is Beaujolais. This is divided into the standard Beaujolais AC, Beaujolais Supérieur which denotes a slightly higher alcohol content and Beaujolais-Villages - an appéllation controllée (quality control) given to about 40 villages and considered

to be of superior quality.

The most prestigious of these wines bear the name of one of the 10 communes (crus). They are worth noting since you will come across them practically everywhere. They are Saint-Amour, Juliénas, Chénas, Moulin-à-Vent, Fleurie, Chiroubles, Morgon, Brouilly, Côte de Brouilly and Régnié (the most recently created, but least distinguished cru).
These are medium priced red dry fruity wines with the villages and communes especially reliable and should be drunk young and served slightly chilled.

Expect to pay: £1.11-£2.80 for basic Beaujolais AC. £1.90-£5.70 per bottle for Beaujolais- Villages or named Commune.

Midi
(Languedoc Roussillon and Provence)
This region stretches from northeast of Marseilles down to the west of Perpignan bordering Spain. Wines from

this region, such as Minervois and Corbières, represent good value dry reds. The Vin de Pays (sometimes referred to as country wines) of the area offer the best value of all. The label shows the Vin de Pays description followed by the region.

Expect to pay: 60p-£2.30 per bottle and a little more if VDQS (Vins Délimités de Qualité Supérieure) is printed on the label.

Rhône
This area is located south of the Burgundy region and continues due south to the Mediterranean near Marseilles. The region generally produces robust, full bodied wines. There is a standard Côtes du Rhône and a Côtes du Rhône Villages, famous for its dry red wine.If the wine comes from a named village (shown on the label) the chances are it will be better quality but more expensive. Côtes du Rhônes are great with cheese and poultry dishes.Expect to pay:88p-£2.22 for Côtes du Rhône label wines. £2.22-£3.33 for Côtes du Rhône Villages.

Loire
The Loire wine region starts at Nantes on the western Atlantic coast of France and

follows the Loire River east to Orléans where it cuts back southeast to Sancerre. The vast majority of wines produced in this

area are white. The Loire offers a wide variety of wine and all have a certain refreshing quality that comes from its northerly position and the character of the soil.

Among the many well known names from this area are Muscadet, Gros Plant Du Nantais, Pouilly-Fumé and Sancerre all of which are dry whites. The Anjou area is well known for its easy drinking Rosé wines that are so versatile that they can drunk through-out the meal.

The whites are best with fish and salads. Although named wines are generally a better buy, in our experience it is especially true for Muscadet where we recommend either a named or "sur lie". Expect to pay: 88p-£1.66 for Gros Plant. £1.11-£2.44 for Muscadet. £3.88-£4.33) for Sancerre & Pouilly Fumé £1.11-£1.77 for Anjou Rosé wines.

If you prefer a medium dry wine then try the Vouvray at £2.50-£3.50. It is also available as sparkling wine.

Popular Wines

Wines that are popular in Britain are widely available in Calais and of course at cheaper prices. Here is a guide to the savings.

Prices obtained from Tesco, Sainsbury's and Oddbins

	France	UK
Banrock Station Chardonnay	£2.99	£4.99
Barossa Cabernet Sauvignon	£6.95	£7.99
Barossa Shiraz	£5.49	£6.99
Barossa Semillon	£3.69	£5.49
Blue Nun	£1.86	£3.00
Barramundi Semillon Chardonnay	£1.79	£4.00
Brown Brothers Late Harvest Muscat 2001	£4.25	£6.86
E &J Gallo, Turning Leaf Cabernet Sauvignon	£4.50	£6.45
E&J Gallo Colombard White	£2.30	£4.50
Errazuriz Chardonnay 2001	£3.58	£5.99
Errazuriz Merlot	£3.58	£5.99
Fetzer Echo Ridge Sauvignon Blanc	£3.78	£5.99
Goats do Roam White	£3.19	£4.00
Goats do Roam Red	£3.19	£4.99
Hardy's Notttage Hill Chardonnay 1999	£2.80	£5.00
Hardy's Nottage Hill Shiraz	£4.09	£5.99
Hardy's Stamp cabernet Merlot	£3.29	£4.99
Jacob's Creek Merlot	£4.39	£5.99
Jacob's Creek Cabernet Sauvingon	£4.48	£5.99
Jacobs Creek Shiraz Cabernet	£3.55	£4.40
Jacobs Creek Semillon Chardonnay	£2.85	£4.35
Lindeman Bin 45 Cabernet Sauvignon	£4.65	£5.99
Lindemans Bin 50 Shiraz	£4.29	£5.99
Lindeman Shiraz Bin 50	£3.96	£5.99

Popular Wines

	France	UK
Nottage Hill Shiraz Cabenet Sauvignon	£2.92	£4.99
Mouton Cadet Red Baron Rothschild	£4.30	£6.99
Mouton Cadet White Baron Rothschild	£4.30	£6.50
Oxford Landing Cabernet Sauvignon	£2.99	£4.40
Oxford Landing Chardonnay	£3.20	£5.00
Penfold's Koonunga Hill	£4.71	£6.99
Penfold's Rawson's Rereat Bin 35	£3.96	£5.99
Pepper Tree Shiraz	£5.99	£7.99
Peter Lehman Semillon	£4.72	£5.49
Paul Mason White	£2.35	£3.70
Paul Mason Red	£2.55	£3.99
Piat D'Or White	£1.99	£3.58
Piat D'Or Red	£1.92	£3.58
Rawsons Retreat Bin 35 Shiraz Cabernet Ruby	£3.99	£5.99
Reynolds Moonshdow Chardonnay	£6.99	£899
Rosemount Estate Cabernet Merlot	£5.09	£6.99
Rosemount Estate Cbernet Sauvignon	£5.39	£7.49
Rosemount Estate Grenache Shiraz	£4.89	£6.99
Rosemount Estate Shiraz Cabernet	£4.99	£6.99
Stowells Sauvignon Blanc	£1.88	£3.76
Tim Adams Semillon	£5.66	£7.59
Wolf Blass Shiraz	£4.99	£6.99
Wolf Blass Red Label	£4.53	£6.49

On special occasions only a bottle of bubbly will do. There's something about popping corks and drinking bubbles that makes a celebration. But does it have to be Champagne?

The Champagne region of France is undoubtedly the most famous and has done more for promoting awareness for sparkling wine than any other region in the world.

In fact, the marketing is so good that some people even refer to all sparkling wine as Champagne. However, any sparkling wine mad e outside the Champagne region, is simply sparkling wine.

Yet, sparkling wine has been made outside the Champagne region since 1820, but the 50 or so sparkling wine appellations get unfairly overlooked.

These appellations include Alsace, Burgundy, the tiny region of Die, Limoux and Saumur in the Loire.

Alsace
The sparkling wine from Alsace is known as **Crémant d'Alsace**, the first French sparkling wine appellation to use the term crémant to mean sparkling in 1976. The industry in Alsace was established by Dopff in 1900 and Wolfberger and Laugel followed shortly. The most popular style is Pinot Blanc however, if you like rosé flavours, try the **Crémant rosé** and enjoy subtle strawberry and cherry flavours. If you do buy these wines, do drink

them within 18 months.

Burgundy (Bourgogne)
Sparkling wines from this region are known as **Crémant de Bourgogne**, although in more recent times the bottle will have the term **Bourgogne Mousseux**.

Though generally good, quality can be variable because producers tend to buy the grapes that have been rejected for use in non-sparkling Burgundy on the cheap. Nevertheless, if you don't mind taking a risk, this wine generally tends to be a bargain. Expect to pay between £3-£4.00 per bottle.

Die
Wines from this

area are labelled as **Clairette de Die Méthode Diose Ancestrale**. These are gorgeously sweet and a bargain for those who have a sweet tooth. Expect to pay around £3.50 a bottle in either Auchan or Carrefour hypermarkets

Limoux
This sunny region somehow produces exceptionally good sparkling wines, despite

the high levels of sunshine it receives. Look out for **Crémant de Limoux** and **Blanquette de Limoux** and expect to pay £2.80 a bottle.

The Loire
Saumur, in The Loire, is the largest French sparkling wine

appellation outside of Champagne. The region produces sparkling **Vouvray** but this is quite hard to find, although the hypermarkets do stock this. **Touraine** and **Crémant de Loire**, when good, can be really good value for money. Expect to pay around £4.50.

Look for the French sparkling wines in the well-stocked shelves of the hypermarkets

Of course sparkling wines come from all around the world. Look for them in British owned outlets.

Italy

Probably the most famous sparkling wine from Italy is the sweet Asti, costing a fraction of the price of demi-sec Champagne and all together better quality. If you prefer something a little drier go for DOCG, brut style sparkling wine.

Spain

The term Cava describes sparkling wine produced in Spain. Spain is the second largest bottle-fermented sparkling wine appellation and mostly known for **Codorniu** and **Freixenet**. This is noteworthy as the method is known as méthode champenoise (made in the Champagne method). Expect to pay around £4.70 per bottle.

California

Prohibition in 1920 put a full stop to the development of sparkling wine in California. Though this was repealed in 1933, the industry did not recover until 1973 when Moët & Chandon chose the Napa Valley to produce its first premium quality winery outside of Champagne: **Mumm Cuvée Napa.**

In the 1980s, the two Spanish houses, Codorniu and Freixenet also invested here. The best California sparkling wine regions are **Mendocino**, **Carneros** and **Sonoma**.

Australia
Australia's sparkling wine industry has grown out of a number of mergers and flown-in talent. From all this industrious activity wines such as **Seppelt Great Western** - now dominates the industry - and **Seaview** were borne.

New Zealand
New Zealand was a little slower than others to create a serious business out of sparkling wine. That is until 1981 when the giant company Montana launched **Lindauer**.

A guide to average savings on sparkling wines

	France	UK
Alsace Crémant Blanc de Blanc	£2.29	£6.00
Asti	£3.14	£6.94
Crémant de Bourgogne	£3.60	£7.49
Banrock Sparkling Shiraz	£5.49	£7.99
Blanquette de Limoux	£2.70	£6.00
Codorniu Classico Cava	£2.79	£5.70
Clairette De Die	£3.15	£6.00
Freixenet	£3.99	£6.99
Green Point Brut	£8.03	£11.99
Hardy's Stamp Chardonnay Pinot Noir Brut	£3.99	£6.49
Kumala Sparkling	£4.99	£6.99
Lindauer Brut	£4.52	£7.99
Lindauer Rosé	£4.52	£7.99
Lindauer Special Reserve NV	£5.98	£8.90
Montana Lindauer Brut	£5.49	£7.99
Mumm Cuvée Napa Brut	£8.49	£10.99
Saumur	£3.69	£5.80
Seaview Brut NV	£3.78	£6.99
Seppelt Great Western Brut NV	£3.78	£6.49

Champagne Charlies?

"I am drinking stars"
Dom Perignon
describing his sparkling wine

The most luxurious drink in the world, sparkling wine, suggests celebration - something special. Situated northeast of Paris with Reims and Epernay at the heart, Champagne is renowned for its sparkling wine.

The climate, the soil, the art of the wine maker and, of course, the grapes all combine to make champagne the most celebrated in terms of unmatched quality and reputation.

These are usually sold under a brand name e.g. Bollinger, Moët et Chandon, Mumm, Veuve Clicquot etc which are nearly always dry. If you do not like dry wines, then ask for a demi-sec or even a rosé champagne.

Only wine made in the champagne area is entitled to be called Champagne.

Other wines of this type is referred to as "sparkling" wine. Some have Méthode Traditionnelle on the label which means made in the "Champagne method".

Expect to pay: £5.90-£7.77 for lesser known brands. £12.00 upwards for the well-known brands.

Champagne comes in the following sizes	
Quart:	20cl
Half-bottle:	37.5cl
Bottle:	75cl
Magnum:	2 bottles
Jeroboam:	4 bottles
Mathusalah:	8 bottles
Salmanazar	12 bottles
Balthazar:	16 bottles
Nebuchadnezzar:	20 bottles

> *"Remember gentleman, it's not just France we are fighting for, it's champagne!"*
>
> **Winston S Churchill, 1918**

Never has so much been said by so many about just one style of wine. It seems everyone loves to drink champagne and that includes the Brits. But why are we being charged so much more than the French for the pleasure?

The reason is simply because they can. But who are "they"? Perhaps "they" are the champagne houses, who seem to have a unique pricing policy for each country. Are they charging our retailers higher prices who in turn are inevitably forced to pass on the cost? One source claims the difference is exchange-rate driven. It's a grey area and no one is rushing to make it black and white.

Nevertheless, while the status quo remains, you can save on average £6.50 a bottle. If you were to buy to the 75 bottles limit of bubbly allowed by Customs & Excise for a wedding or celebration you will have made a massive saving of £487.50! Now that is something to celebrate.

Champagne	Av.UK	Av.France
Bolinger	£28.00	£17.24
Canard Duchêne	£15.50	£10.90
Deutz Blanc de Blancs	£21.99	£8.98
Krug Grande Cuvée	£73.00	£55.00
Lanson Black Label	£20.99	£12.50
Laurent Perrier	£21.00	£14.00
Mercier Brut	£17.00	£12.50
Moët et Chandon	£20.99	£16.00
Mumm Cordon Rouge	£19.49	£15.50
Nicolas Feuillate	£16.99	£ 9.50
Piper Heidsieck	£18.99	£13.00
Veuve Clicquot Ponsardin	£23.00	£16.20

Without a doubt, the best bargain to be had in France is the beer. With savings of up to 50 per cent beer drinkers are certainly not bitter !

Fortunately, beer is stocked in abundance across the Channel and the most widely available beers tend to be continental. The average continental beer has an alcoholic content of at least 4.5% which is more than 1% stronger than the average British bitter.

You may find 'promos' offering beers cheaply but these could be lower alcohol beers such as Kœnigsbier or Brandeberg. These retail at around £2.80 for 24 bottles but have an alcoholic volume of only 2.80%.

The majority of continental beers are light in colour and are best served chilled. They are sold in 25cl bottles which equates to just under half a pint (0.43).

The highest alcoholic beers tend to be from Belgium. The more popular ones include Hoegaarden (5% ABV) known as Witbier or Bière Blanche meaning white beer and refers to its naturally cloudy appearance. Although in Britain cloudiness is usually associated with the beer being past its best, in this case it is due to its production process and ingredients: barley, unmalted wheat, Styrian and Kent hops, coriander and çuraçao. As it brews, the top-fermenting yeast turns the malt to alcohol, but because the wheat is not malted, the starches contribute to the final cloudy appearance.

Possibly the best known Belgian beers are Trappist beers made by monks in just 5 monasteries in Belgium. These include Chimay Red (7%) - copper colour and slightly sweet, Chimay White (6.3%) - lots of hop and slightly acidic, Chimay Blue (7.1%) - fruity aromas, Orval (6.2%) - orange hue, with acidity; Rochefort 6,8,10 (ABVs are 7.3%, 7.5% and 11.3%) - characteristics range from russet colour with a herbal palate, tawny and fruity to dark brown with chocolate and fruity palate respectively.

Pilsner-style beers include the mass marketed beers of Jupiler, a dry and soft easy drinking example and Stella Artois (the biggest brewing company in Belgium) who also make Leffe - an abbey style ale.

France itself has two brewing regions. The first is in the north around the city of Lille, the most well known part being French Flanders. The style of beer produced - bière de garde - resembles its Belgian counterparts. Strasbourg, in the east is the other brewing region. The final product is similar to German lagers.

The major French breweries are Kronenbourg/Kanterbrau, Mutzig and Pelforth. The latter, situated near Lille,

produces light and dark lagers: Pelforth Blonde (5.8%) and Pelforth Brune (5.2% & 6.5%).

There are also popular beers from Australia such as Castlemain XXXX and the sweetish Fosters lager (both 4%) which are widely available.

Products from many British breweries also share shelf space in northern France, especially at British supermarkets such as Tesco and Sainsbury's. These include Shepherd Neame's malty Bishop's Finger (12.5%), John Smith's bitter (4.8% & 4%), Whitbread's creamy headed Boddington's bitter (3.8%), Tetley's creamy, nutty Yorkshire ale (3.6%) and Ireland's earthy, dry Guinness Draught (5%).

Whichever beer you choose your enjoyment will be enhanced by the knowledge that it often costs only half of what you would have paid in the UK!

Here For The Beer?

**Yes It's True -
Beer from 12p per 25cl Bottle!
Most outlets carry continental beers
Here's a selection**

Beer	% Vol	Av. £ Price	
Munsterbrau	4.7	12p	Auchan
Blondy	5.0	13p	Pidou
Nordik Pils	5.0	13p	Pidou
Blondebrau	4.6	13p	Pidou
Seumeuse	5.0	14p	Sainsbury's
St Omer 50cl cans per 25cl	5.0	17p	Widely available
Sterling	4.9	15	Auchan
ESP	5.2	17p	Eastenders
Kanterbrau	4.7	18/19p	Widely available
Meteor Biere D'Alsace	5.0	20p	Auchan
Kronenbourg	4.7	21 p	Widely available
Stella Artois	5.2	23p	Widely available
ESP	9.2	24p	Eastenders
Amsterdam Mariner 33cl	5.0	26p	Widely available
33 Export	5.0	28p	Widely available
Grölsch	5.0	29p	Widely available
1664	6.3	30p	Widely available

Some Popular Beers

Beer	Auchan	Carrefour	Pidou	Sainsbury'	Tesco	Cheers
1664 24 x 50cl					£14.43	
Amsterdam Mariner 24 x 50cl					£13.64	
Beck's 24 x 50cl	£16.35	£16.75			£13.35	
Becks 24 x 33cl			£13.68			£11.50
Blondy 24 x 25cl			£12.50			£ 2.99
Boddingtons 24 x 44cl		£20.70	£14.40			£13.50
Budweiser 20 x 50cl			£11.70		£11.90	
Caffreys 24 x 50cl					£12.95	
Carling Black Label 24 x 50cl	£12.90		£12.96	£11.95	£11.34	
Carlsberg Special Brew 24 x 50cl	£21.40	£20.00	£20.20	£20.00		
Foster Lager 24 x 50cl	£14.00		£12.99	£12.99	£12.76	
Grolsch 24 x 50cl	£13.60			£11.20	£ 9.89	£11.90
Guinness 24 x 50cl					£19.80	
Heineken 24 x 44cl					£19.10	
Hoegaarden White 24 x 33cl *25cl			*£9.80			£11.25
Kanterbrau 24 x 5cl					£ 3.72	
Kronenourg 24 x 50cl					£10.72	£10.50
Nastro Azurro Lager 24 x 33cl			£11.00	£11.79	£11.02	
Ruddles County 24 x 50cl				£19.49		
Saint Omer 24 x 50cl		£8.52			£ 6.70	£ 6.85
Stella Artois 24 x 50cl			£12.00	£12.06	£11.35	£11.45
Stella 24 x 25cl						
Tanglefoot 24 x 50cl	£14.00		£13.00	£14.85	£13.22	£ 4.89

Channel Shoppers generally think of Calais as an ideal place to buy wine and beer. But don't forget there are great savings on Spirits too!

Though Northern France does not produce any wine it does have very fertile land, ideal for growing hops and cereals for beer and also for producing what they fondly refer to as 'eau de vie'; France's very own tipple: Genièvre. The juniper berry is the principal ingredient creating a highly distinctive style of gin. The exact nature of the recipe is a closely guarded secret by all three distilleries in Houlle, near to St Omer, Wambrechies and in Loos near to Lille, each proudly producing gin with subtle differences. If you would like to taste Genièvre you can find it at the hypermarkets with an alcoholic content of up to 49%! Expect to pay between £7.00-£8.00 per bottle.

Whatever your favourite tipple, you are most likely to find it either at the hypermarkets or at Tesco and Sainsbury's. The following tipple table is a guide to what's available and where.

Savings range from £2-£5. For instance a 1 litre bottle of Famous Grouse costs £16.99 in UK Sainsbury's and just £12.79 in their Calais branch; that's a saving of £4.20!

Gienievre made in Loos

That's The Spirit - The Tipple Table

100 of the most popular products in alphabetical order. Where possible we have included the average UK price so that you can see your savings at a glance. Prices have been converted to sterling. Prices tend to fluctuate, usually within a 5% band.

TIPPLE TABLE - PRICES ARE IN £ STERLING

PRODUCT	% vol	Ave UK price	Auchan	Carrefour	Sainsbury	Tesco
Aberlour Scotch Whisky 10yrs 70cl	43	19.99	11.62	12.09	13.99	12.70
Absolut Vodka 70cl	40	13.09	8.55		11.10	13.70
Bacardi White Rum 1L	37.5	14.99	10.30	10.30	11.49	10.00
Baileys Irish Cream 70cl	17	16.95	7.65	7.36	10.95	10.50
Ballantines 70cl	40		8.20	8.70		
Beefeater London Dry Gin 70cl	40	12.44	8.28			9.80
Bells *70d 1L	40	16.49	8.81*		12.49	11.50
Benedictine 70cl	40	16.99	10.68	10.61		
Black & White Scotch Whisky 70cl	40		6.88	7.36		
Bombay Sapphire London Dry Gin 70cl	40	12.99	10.70			9.50
Calvados 70cl	40			8.44		
Campari 1L	25	16.15	8.90	9.06	8.99	8.66
Canadian Club Whisky 70c	40	14.99	7.13	7.61	9.99	9.69
Canadian Mist Whisky 70cl	40		6.80			7.12
Captain Morgan 1L	40	16.99				10.59
Cardhu Single Malt 70cl	40	17.22	18.00			
Chivas Regal Scotch Whisky 12 yrs 70cl	40	19.99	14.87	14.88	15.95	14.90
Cinzano Bianco 1L *75cl	16	*4.99	4.07			3.90
Cinzano Rosso 1L	16		3.87	3.90		
Clan Campbell 70cl	40		7.21	7.52		
Clès Des Ducs Armagnac 70cl	40		8.72	8.67		11.22
Cointreau 70cl	40	16.18	9.30	10.07	9.05	9.10
Courvoisier Cognac 70cl	40	20.34	14.60			13.20
Croft Tawny Port 75cl	19.5		5.40			
Cutty Sark Scotch Whisky 70cl	40		8.00	8.37		
Dimple 70cl	40		17.57	15.93		
Drambuie 70cl	40	14.99	18.88		11.49	15.80
Dubonnet 1L	16	7.48	4.54	4.88		

That's The Spirit - The Tipple Table

PRODUCT	% vol	Ave UK price	Auchan	Carrefour	Sainsbury	Tesco
Famous Grouse Scotch Whisky 70cl *1L	40	16.99	8.85	9.30	12.99*	8.91
Four Roses Bourbon Scotch Whisky 70cl	40		8.24	8.55		
Gilbey's London Dry Gin 70cl	37.5		6.00	6.33		
Glen Rogers Scotch Whisky 8yrs 70cl	40		8.86	8.88		
Glen Turner Pure Malt 8yrs 70cl	40		9.18	9.26		
Glenfiddich 70cl	40	21.10	12.72	13.00		13.00
Glenlivet 12 yrs 70cl	40	19.99	15.78	15.78		14.80
Glenmorangie 10yrs 70cl	40	22.99	17.20	17.71	17.99	15.80
Gold River 8yrs 70cl	30			6.43		
Gordon's London Dry Gin 1L	37.5	15.48	9.98	10.10	10.99	11.00
Grand Marnier Liqueur 70cl	40	14.29	10.44	11.07	10.29	15.80
Grants Whisky 70cl	40	15.39	7.00	7.00	9.99	7.10
Haig Gold Label 70cl	40		6.94			
Harveys Bristol Cream 1L	17.5	7.89				6.70
Hennessy Cognac 1L *70cl	40		14.82	20.44		
J&B Whisky 70cl	40	14.99	8.72		11.99	11.90
Jack Daniels Whiskey 70cl	43	17.29	10.95	11.48	11.90	14.50
Jameson Irish Whiskey 70cl	40	13.99	8.78		10.99	9.27
Janneau Grand Armagnac 1L * 70cl	40	*9.44	12.24			
Jim Bean Bourbon 70cl	40	14.44	9.20	9.46	10.99	9.50
Johnnie Walker Black Label 70cl	40	16.49	11.92		14.95	14.50
Johnnie Walker Red Label 1L	40	16.90	8.24	10.98	14.94	
Kahlua Liqueur 70cl	26	12.99	9.62		9.59	8.00
Knockando Whisky 70cl	43	19.99	19.90		14.99	
Label 5 70cl	40		6.79	7.15		
Lambs Navy Rum 70cl	40	11.95			8.95	8.50
Laphroaig 70cl	43	22.99			18.99	16.60
Laphroaig 10 yrs 70cl	40		17.78			
Long John Scotch Whisky 70cl	40		6.69	7.13		
MacAllan 70cl	43	22.99	21.17	21.17	17.49	16.00
MacArthur's 70cl	40		9.99			
Malibu white rum 1L 70cl	21	15.49	8.50	*6.22	9.49	9.50

That's The Spirit - The Tipple Table

PPRODUCT	% vol	Ave UK price	Auchan	Carrefour	Sainsbury	Tesco
Martell 3 Star Cognac 70cl	40	25.49	12.74	13.45		12.50
Martini Bianco 1L	16	5.99	4.92	4.90		4.97
Martini Rosé 1L	16	5.99	5.48	5.40		4.94
Martini Rosso 1L	16	5.99	4.70	4.82		4.94
Negrita Rum 1L	40		5.15	7.10		
Noilly Prat 1L *75cl	18	*5.99	5.56	5.55		5.54
Old Lady's London Dry Gin 70cl	37.5		6.75	5.66		
Old Virginia Bourbon 70cl	40		7.64	7.65		
Pastis 51 1L	45		6.64	7.30		
Pernod 1L *75cl	15	13.99	10.59	10.52	9.99	11.55
Pimms 70cl	25	15.99	7.60	7.18	9.99	10.49
Remy Martin VSOP 70cl	40	26.18	17.73	18.64		17.40
Ricard Pastis 70cl	45		9.87	10.50		
Sandeman Port 75cl	19		6.00	5.50		
Smirnoff Vodka 70cl	37.5	13.99	7.85	7.05	10.99	10.80
St James White Rum 70CL	40		7.33	6.80		
Southern Comfort 70cl	40	14.99	10.17	10.12		11.00
Stones Original Ginger Wine 70cl	n/a	5.19				4.69
Teachers Scotch Whisky 70cl	40	11.69	8.83	7.90		8.87
Tia Maria 70cl *50	26.5	18.99	*6.90	9.35	12.99	12.61
Vladivar Vodka 1L	37.5	13.64				8.64
Warninks Advocaat 70cl	17.2	9.99				7.66
White Horse Scotch Whisky 70cl	40	10.99				8.37
Whyte & Mackay Special Reserve 70cl	40	11.29	7.34	7.36		
Wild Turkey No.8 Bourbon Whisky 70cl	43.4		9.00	9.56		
William Lawson Scotch Whisky 70cl *1L	40		7.95	7.51		
William Peel 70cl *1L	40		*11.90	6.78		
Wyborowa Vodka 70cl	40		7.54			
Zubrowka Vodka 70cl	40		9.02	85.65		

The Epicurean's Tour of The Shops

When shopping in any French town what stands out is the variety of traditional gastronomic shops, some of which have no comparable counterpart in the UK. It may be a cultural thing but, very simply, the French like to specialise.

Take the Boucherie for example - the butcher. The Boucherie sells all types of meat and poultry - except pork. To buy pork you need to visit the Charcuterie - which means cooked meat.

The Charcuterie, originally a pork butcher, has evolved into a pork-based delicatessen. Visiting a Charcuterie for the first time will shift your perception of the humble pig "le cochon' in gastronomic terms for ever! Now you will see it as pâté, terrine, rillettes, rillons, hams, dried sausages, fresh sausages, pieds de porc, andouillettes, boudins noirs et blancs. This pork lover's haven also offers ready made pork meals with a selection of plats du jour

that just need heating up when you get home.

Horse meat is also popular in France and this is sold in outlets known as Boucherie Chevaline - horse meat butcher, generally identifiable by a horse's head sign.

Cheese, a much revered commodity in France, is produced with exacting procedures by the highly skilled maître fromager (master cheese specialist). The shop to visit to get the feel of the cheese culture at its best is the Fromagerie - a specialist cheese shop which will probably have around 300 varieties on sale.

A cross between a grocery store and a delicatessen is the Epicerie. The store sells cheese and fresh meat among other food products. These days the Epricerie is based a little on the Supermarché and an Alimentation Général - a general store - and has lost some of its authenticity.

Calais and Boulogne both being fishing towns are awash with fresh seafood. You can buy the catch of the day from the Poissonerie. This could be a fishmonger or just a stall.

Another example of specialisation in action is the Boulangerie - the bakery. The shelves are stacked with all types of unusual bread and buns and occasionally cakes and quiches too.

But for a fiendishly good selection of cakes and biscuits, it is over to the Pâtisserie for specialist cake, flans and tarts. The Pâtisserie sometimes sells ice cream too.

Sweets, not the commercial pre-wrapped type, but handmade sweets such as bon-bons, nougat and crystallised fruit, have their own home in a Confiserie or Chocolaterie - a high class sweet or chocolate shop. The products are a little pricey but good quality, delicious and beautifully packaged.

For fresh fruit, flowers and vegetables and fresh French delights the best place is the Marché - outdoor market. These are generally open on a Saturday or Wednesday.

You could of course by-pass the specialist shops which offer pleasant insightful echoes of French daily life and culture - a shopping experience unlike any you can have in the UK. You could, instead, shop in one of the immense Hypermarché - hypermarkets. The total anonymity that comes with being one of hundreds of trolley pushers walking around thousands of kilometres of floor space in a state of suspended reality is an experience all of its own!

Say Cheese

Take a glass of your favourite wine, break off a piece of baguette, fill it with your favourite cheese - voila! a slice of French culture.

The inherent passion for wine within the French culture is closely followed by a love for cheese, so much so that France has become renowned for its remarkably large selection of cheeses. Incredibly, the number of different varieties is believed to be in excess of 700. Not only do supermarkets dedicate large areas of floor space to their cheese counters, but the French also have specialist cheese shops.

These quaint shops are called Fromageries offering cheese in all its colours and consistencies.

Though nasal passages have to grapple with the pungent aroma that hangs heavily in the air, the palate can look forward to a delightful epicurean experience. It is at the fromagerie that the finest cheeses can be found, thanks to the resident maître fromager. His highly skilled job combines the complexities of cheese selection, storage and the delicate process of "affinage'. This is the art of ageing a young cheese to maturity so that it is offered in its prime.

To the uninitiated though, the cheese counter must look like a daunting display of yellow and white hues with the odd shout of blue. No matter how tempting these colours look, one wonders about the taste. Fortunately, it is customary for supermarkets and fromageries to offer dégustation (sampling) upon request.

Fromageries to try are:

La Maison du Fromage, 1 rue Andre-Gerschel, Calais

La Cave du Fromager, 23 rue de Lille. Boulogne

Cremerie La Ferme at 22 rue Poincaré. Dunkirk

Say Cheese

Boulogne is favoured with **Phillippe Oliver's** cheese shop at 43 rue Thiers, reputedly the most famous cheese vendor in the world. A visit here is a must for any cheese lover.

Although it is not possible to list all available cheeses, some will already be familiar to you, such as Normandy's camembert and brie from Ile de France (especially the President label) are widely found and at a third less than UK prices. Fromages fermiers (farmhouse cheese) are considered to be the finest of all. These are made by small producers using milk from their own farm animals. When unpasteurised milk is used this is denoted with the words "lait cru'. Other varieties to try are:

Le Brin. A small hexagon shaped cheese. Made from cow's milk, it is mild and creamy. The edible rind has a delicate, pleasant aroma. The special method of production leaves the cheese high in calcium and phosphorus.

Cantorel Roquefort. A speciality of southwest France, this blue cheese is ripened in the caves of Cambalou for at least 90 days in accordance with its Appellation d'Origine Contrôlée. Made entirely from sheep's milk, its distinctive taste is best enjoyed with Barsac or Sauternes wines.

Chimay. You may already be familiar with the Belgian Trappist beer of this name. Chimay is also a range of six Belgian Trappist cheeses. Chimay Bière is flavoured with the beer and is a treat for the palate.

Rambol. Decorated with walnuts it looks like a small gâteau and is smooth with a mellow flavour.

Société Roquefort. Creamy in texture and distinguished by its marbled green and ivory colouring.

St Agur. A creamy blue veined cheese from the Auvergne. It has a mild flavour and sits well on a cheese board.

Say Cheese

Tartare. A cream cheese spread from Périgord made with garlic and herbs. It comes as a full fat cheese and for slimmers there's Tartare Light with just a third of the calorie content.

Trappe de Belval. Made by nuns at the abbey of Belval located near Hesdin. It has a rather hard exterior concealing a creamy and mild interior.

Serving suggestions:

• Cheese is at its best served at room temperature. Remove from the fridge at least one hour before eating .

• Allow 2oz per person for a cheese board and 4oz per person for a cheese and wine evening.

• Select 3-4 different types of cheese for an attractive display, especially on a cheese board.

Storage Tips:

Fortunately, most hard cheeses can be frozen as long as they are not overmature.This is not recommended for soft cheeses.

Generally, the following guidelines for fridge storage apply:

• Fresh Cheese (soft cheese): Eat within a few days.
• Blue Cheese Can be kept up to three weeks.
• Goat's Ewe's Milk Cheese: Will keep for up to two weeks.
• Always store cheese in the lowest part of the fridge wrapped in foil or in an air proof container to prevent drying out.

Eau, What A Choice!

It's the best thirst quenching drink there is. It's not alcohol but it's a bargain !

Mineral water (eau minérale) both still (plate) and sparkling (gazeuse) is exceptionally good value for money and substantially cheaper to buy in France. Why this is so is perplexing as unlike alcohol, there is no tax to blame.

There is often a vast selection of different brands at the hypermarkets. Some, such as Evian, Volvic and the comparatively expensive Perrier will be familiar, yet some of the lesser known brands are just as good. For example the sparkling River brand is just 18p for 1.5 litres which we believe to be under half the price of the equivalent in the UK and Lucheux - which at 12.5p a 2- litre bottle must merit some space in your boot.

In our blind tasting, we sampled some mineral waters at fridge temperature. Here are a selection of commonly available waters:

Badoit: Slightly sparkling from the Loire.
Ave Price: 35p 1L Comment: Slightly salty

Contrexéville: From Vosges. Reputedly good for the kidneys. Has a slightly diuretic effect.
Ave Price: 3p) 1.5L Comment: Slightly salty.

Evian: From the town of Evian on Lake Geneva.It has a slightly diuretic effect.
Ave Price: 42p 2L Comment: Tasteless but thirst quenching.

Perrier: A well marketed mineral water from Nîmes. Full of sparkle and is generally used as soda water in France.
Ave Price: 45p 1L Comment: Most refreshing with almost no flavour.

River: Sparkling water
Ave Price:18p 1.5L
Comment: Slightly chalky on the palate.

Vichy: A sparkler from Vichy.
Ave Price: 30p 1.5L Comment: Like bicarbonate of soda.

Vittel: A still yet rugged mineral water from Nancy.
Ave Price: 28p 1.5L Comment: Refreshing and slightly sweet.

Volvic: A still water from the Auvergne filtered through volcanic rock.
Ave Price: 30p 1.5L
Comment: Smooth silky taste.

French Bread

It's the law! Every French village must have its own boulangerie (bakery) supplying the villagers with freshly baked bread every day of the week.

Governed by French law, the boulangerie emerges as the single most important shop in any village, faithfully providing the residents with an essential part of their staple diet - bread.

As with all things French an etiquette has evolved around bread. It is generally considered unacceptable to serve bread purchased in the morning in the evening. No self-respecting Frenchman would dare to insult his guests in this way!

However, left-over bread may be used perhaps for dunking in hot chocolate - in specially formulated wide cups - or alternatively can be cooked in soup.

Boulangerie at Carrefour

The most famous and popular French bread (both within and outside France) is the long, thin baguette or French stick. It is uniform in length and its weight - governed by French law - must be 250 grams!

Although the baguette is made simply from soft flour, yeast, water and a pinch or two of salt, it has an appealing fluffy texture and can be enjoyed just as well on its own as it can with food. However, its short life span means that it must be consumed soon after it has been baked. Bakeries routinely bake bread twice a day to ensure fresh loaves for a very discriminating public.

Variations on the baguette include the ficelle

(which means string). It is the thinnest loaf available. In contrast un pain or Pariesen is double the size of a baguette. A compromise is reached with petit pains and the bâtons which are much shorter than the baguette and similar to large rolls. For breakfast (le petit dèjeuner) the French will also enjoy a continental breakfast (better known in France as viennoiserie). This includes such delicious treats as the famous pastry-style croissant. This familiar crescent-shaped roll was Marie Antoinett's inadvertent contribution to western breakfast culture. She introduced them to Parisien

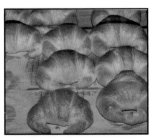

The shap of croissant is based on the Ottoman flag

royals in the late 18th century where they proved to be an epicurean hit.

In Marie Antoinette's home country of Vienna, however, the croissant had been making a regular appearance at the breakfast table as early as 1683. It was in this year that the Polish army saved the city from Turkish hands and in celebration the Viennese baked a crescent-shaped creation based on the Ottoman flag - voila, the croissant was born!

The croissant is similar to puff pastry - made with yeast dough and butter and is usually accompanied by confit (crystallised fruit) or confiture (various flavours of jam). Sometimes it is served with jam, cheese or chocolate and can be savoured hot or cold.

Traditionally, the croissant is dunked by the French into their coffee in wide cups designed for this purpose.

French Bread

This French idiosyncrasy can also be traced back to the late 17th century. The defeated Turks had left some sacks of coffee beans before they left Vienna. These were discovered by a group of Armenian Jews who started the croissant dunking tradition.

There are also many other tempting and unusual styles of bread available at the specialist boulangerie (bakery) or the boulangerie counter of the hypermarket.

Here are some suggestions you may like to try:

Pain au chocolat. A croissant style bun imbued with chocolate (delicious when warm).

Brioche. A breakfast bun made from yeast, dough, eggs and butter, giving it a wonderful sweet, buttery aroma and taste.

Couronnes. A baguette style bread in the shape of a ring.

Pain aux noix. An outstanding bread baked with walnuts on the inside and on the crust.

Pain aux olives. A delicious bread with olives and olive oil.

Pain de sègle. Made with rye and wheat.

Pain noir. Wholemeal bread.

Pain de son. Wholemeal bread fortified with bran.

Pain de mie. Sliced bread with a soft crust. Used for sandwiches.

Pain biologique. This bread is baked with organic wholemeal flour.

Pain campagne. Flatter than a baguette but also heavier. it has the advantage of staying fresh for longer.

Pain au Levain/Pain à l'ancienne. Both these names refer to French bread made from sour dough. This is probably one of the oldest styles of French bread.

Specialities at the Pâtisserie

If, like the French, you have a sweet tooth then a visit to a pâtisserie gives a whole new meaning to the phrase "Let Them Eat Cake".

In true French style, even the last course of a meal is not the least. Dinner in any French home will always conclude with a sweet, which if it is not home made, will be bought from the pâtisserie - a specialist cake shop. The pâtisserie may also have a selection of handmade confectionary.

Like French wines and cheese, different areas of France have their own regional indulgences on offer. For instance, from Provence come Marrons Glacés and Fruits Glacés: the former is an autumnal treat of chestnuts in vanilla-flavoured syrup; the latter is fresh fruit in sugar syrup.

Normandy, famous for its apple orchards, offers Tarte Normande. A variation is Gratin de Pommes Vallée D'Auge - it is no ordinary apple crumble; it is soaked in calvados (an apple brandy produced in Normandy) and then baked in crème fraîche. The Pas de Calais also has an indigenous tart whose thick pastry has led to the name Tarte au Gros Bord. It is adorned simply with custard and sugar.

Other offerings include:

Anglois
A simple plum tart.

Biscuit de Reims
A small oblong shaped macaroon from Reims.

Galopin
A thick pancake sprinkled with sugar.

Gaufres à la Flamande
Waffles powdered with sugar and sometimes served with whipped cream.

Pain d'épices
A spicey honey cake.

Specialities at the Pâtisserie

Rabote
A whole apple cooked in pastry.

Tarte au Fromage
Cheese cake made from eggs and cottage cheese.

Nougat Glacé
From Provence a frozen honey and almond desert.

Pastis Gascon
Thin pastry, layered between the folds with vanilla sugar and butter, adorned with apple and marinated in armagnac.

Baba au Rhum
A yeast product soaked in rum flavoured syrup. Best eaten with a spoon.

Where to shop for your bread and cakes:

Joly Desenclos
46 rue de Lille
6220 Boulogne sur Mer
Tel: 00 33 (0)321 80 50 52

Fred
Boulevard Jacquard
Calais
Situated near the Town Hall with a tea room.

Pâtisserie Boutteau
19 place Jean-Bart
Dunkerque
Tel: 00 33 (0)328 66 77 81
A family run business established in 1892 with a tea room,

La Croissantine
84 bis, rue St Jean
Le Touquet
Tel: 00 33 (0)321 06 30 50

Tobacco Prices Up In Smoke!

With savings of £2.00 or more on a packet of cigarettes, topping up in France makes sense.

In theory you can buy unlimited amounts of tobacco for personal use both on board the ferries and in France but the "advisory guideline" is a generous 3200 cigarettes. Customs officers tend to apply these guide lines stringently.

In France tobacco and cigarettes can be purchased from outlets called **Tabacs** where prices are state regulated. You can purchase cigarettes in petrol stations too, but they are not regulated here so prices are a little higher.

Unlike supermarkets in the UK, in France, supermarkets or hypermarkets **do not** sell tobacco at all.

Most tabacs are closed on Sundays and bank holidays but most accept credit cards.

Tobacco Prices Up In Smoke!

You can expect savings of around 50% on board the ferries and save a further 5% when you buy them in Tabacs, so you may as well top up in France.

	France	U.K.
Cigarettes	Av. £	Av. £
Benson & Hedges	£2.06	£4.51
Camel	£2.29	£4.51
Dunhill	£2.72	£4.51
Gauloises	£2.46	£4.20
Gitanes	£1.74	£4.51
John Player Special	£1.80	£4.00
Lambert & Butler	£2.23	£4.20
Marlboro	£2.34	£4.51
Rothmans	£2.15	£4.51
Silk Cut	£2.34	£4.51
Superkings	£2.23	£4.00
Tobacco		
Drum 50g	£2.66	£7.00
Golden Virginia 40g	£2.08	£7.47
Old Holborn 40g	£2.34	£7.47
Samson 50g	£2.30	£7.37
Cigars		
King Edward Imperial x 5	£4.00	£8.90
Villager Export x 5	£3.75	£4.60
Hamlet Cigars x 50	£12.58	£27.00

Always ask for a receipt as the Customs Officer may demand to see this.

***Everyone knows about Calais lace.
But did you know this industry was started
by English smugglers?***

According to French chronicles, the first Englishman to smuggle a lace machine into Calais was Robert Webster in 1816. Though the reliability of this reporting cannot be verified, it is a fact that illegal smuggling of lace machines by Englishmen into Calais did take place. In Blighty, Nottingham lace makers were plying their trade by hand. To them, modern technology meant unemployment. Opposition was so bitter that the machines were smuggled to Calais where conditions were more welcoming. The English set up home in terraced houses-cum-workshops in the Calais district of St. Pierre.

Unemployment in the area was high so finding workers was easy. Import taxes were also high so they had little competition from their counterparts in England. Most importantly, the French aristocracy had returned to Calais and loved the luxurious lace.

In fact, the entire industry developed so well in the hands of expatriate Englishmen that Calais become internationally reknowned for its fashionable, quality lace. Even today, a hefty 78% of the lace production in Calais is exported to 140 countries around the world (and 80% of that is made into lingerie!).

The lace industry in Calais is still run by families, many of whom are of English descent. Though they are inherently French, they still eat Christmas pudding and welsh-rarebit.

Other Shopping Ideas - Foie Gras

The Egyptians enjoyed it more than 2000 years ago. So did the ancient Greeks and Roman emperors. The French perfected it into an art form during the last 200 years and now you can enjoy it too.

Foie gras, pronounced *fwah gra*, is a much revered goose liver pâté. It means literally *fat liver*. In winter, the geese are force-fed with corn and grain so that their livers become supple and enlarged to produce large quantities of *foie* - liver.

Foie gras is sometimes augmented with truffles but either way it is available cooked or semi-cooked in tins or jars. The latter condition gives it a longer shelf life in the refrigerator.

Serve it thoroughly chilled but slice it with a warmed knife. Accompany it with toast or baguette and enjoy a truly gastronomic taste of France.

Where to buy foie gras:

L'Epicerie Des Dunes
corner of Faidherbe and Geeraert, Dunkirk Malo
Tel: 00 33 (0)328 63 22 09

Comtesse du Barry
59 Boulevard Jacquard
Calais
Tel: 00 33 (0)321 85 14 13

Comtesse du Barry
35 Grande Rue
Boulogne
Tel: 00 33 (0)321 87 19 20

Marché Plus
70 rue de Metz
Le Touquet
Tel: 00 33 (0)321 05 03 89

Sauternes wine is a divine accompaniment to Foie Gras

Le Shopping Basket

With the pound so strong, shopping in France is altogether cheaper these days.
Here are some shopping comparisons

Le Shopping Basket

Product	Av. France £	Av. UK £
Butter (cheapest brand)	£0.26	£0.72
Brie (1 kilo)	£2.81	£3.12
Petit Filou Fromage Frais x 18pots	£1.50	£2.55
Nutella Chocolate spread 400g	£1.09	£1.66
Long Grain Rice 1kg	£0.54	£1.00
Cous Cous kg	£0.65	£1.20
Pasta 1kg	£0.52	£0.96
Kellogs Cornflakes 375g	£1.00	£1.39
Pork per 1.5kg	£3.74	£5.08
Stewing steak 1kg	£5.50	£6.06
Evian Still water 6 x 1.5L	£0.47	£0.67
Nesquick 430ml	£1.10	£2.49
1 bottle of white wine	£2.00	£4.00
1 x 2L Coca-Cola	£0.85	£1.17
Carte Noir Arabica Coffee 250g	£6.19	£7.89
Lavazza Espresso 250g	£1.65	£1.99
Aluminium Foil 20mx290m	£1.34	£2.09
Kitchen roll (pack of 2 own brand)	£0.70	£1.39
Persil Washing Biological Powder 7.2kg	£8.42	£11.30
Domestos Bleach 75cl	£2.27	£2.69
Cif/Jif Bathroom Cleaning Cream per L	£1.62	£2.50
Ajax Spray bathroom spray 500ml	£1.20	£1.60
Own label dishwasher tablets	£3.04	£4.97
Toilet rolls (pack of 6 own brand)	£1.00	£1.90
Gillette Sensor Razor blades 5pk	£0.32	£0.89
Gillette Sensor Excel Shaving Razor	£2.33	£3.89
Sensodyne toothpaste 75ml	£1.90	£2.50
Two torch batteries	£2.80	£3.49
Totals	**£56.81**	**£81.16**

Other Shopping Ideas

Cider (Cidre)
French supermarkets and some cash & carries, sell both French and UK ciders. There are differences, notably that French cider tends to contain less alcohol, around 2.4% as opposed to 5%+ for the British ciders. British ciders such as Strongbow and Bulmers are generally available in France at about half the UK price.

Chocolate
Chocolate making is a prosperous cottage industry and hand-made chocolates are quite a tasty treat in France.

Olives
In general olives (both black and green) are about 30% cheaper in French supermarkets.

Jam
The French brand of jam, Bonne Maman, has quite a following in the UK. It's cheaper to buy in France. Typically a 340g jar costs 79p in France and £1.35 in the UK.

Mustard (Moutard)
Mustard is substantially cheaper in France and there is a wider selection. Dijon mustard prices start at 22p for 370g jar of Dijon mustard compared to a typical UK price of 59p for 250g. English mustard is slightly hotter. Try seeded Dijon mustard; it has a particularly delicate flavour.

Filtered Coffee (Café Moulu)
This is widely available and at half the UK prices. Try the taste of even the cheapest brands of filtered coffee and you will not be disappointed. A 1kg (4 x 250g pack) can be found for as little as 30p. Try Arabica.

Fruit Juice (Jus de Fruit)
Expect to pay a third less. Brands such as Recre, Goldhorn and Lagona range from 29p-43p per 1L carton. In the UK the price range would be 59p-89p.

Peanuts (Cacahuètes)
Look out for peanuts - 30% cheaper than the UK price!

Chocolate Milkshake Drinks

The Nestlé Nesquik drinks are normally substantially cheaper in all French supermarkets - typically around £2.47 for 1 kilo. In the UK the standard 225gm Nesquik drink retails for around £1 (equivalent to £4 per kilo).This represents a 40% saving on the UK supermarket price.

Fish (Poisson)

If you have enjoyed a fish or seafood meal, you may be inclined to buy your own to take home. The hypermarkets generally have comprehensive fish and seafood sections or better still, visit a fish monger (poissonnerie).

Anchovies

You get a wider selection of anchovies, and at half price in France- good value at the hypermarkets.

Olive Oil (Huile d'olives)

The finest French olive oils - like French wines - come from named origins and even *Appellations Contrôlées* - quality controlled areas.

They have a gentle flavour tempered with slight sweetness and are great as condiments, but not suitable for cooking.

These olive oils have low acidity (sometimes as little as 0.2%) which is significant because acidity affects the rate at which the oil deteriorates. Labels of assured finest quality to look out for are Huile de Provence and Huile d'Olives Nyons (the latter is subject to quality control with its own Appellation d'Origine. This sort of quality is expensive and could be up to £30.00 in the UK (less in France). Generally, you are likely to buy commercially blended brands.

Look for either Extra Virgin (Vierge) or First Cold Pressing (Premier Presson Froid) whose acidity is never more than 1%, but is better still at 0.5%, Fine Virgin olive oil at 1.5% or less, and Ordinary Virgin olive oil whose acidity level is 3%. This sort of quality olive oil in the UK is rarely below £6.00 per litre, yet in France the price is around £3.50.

Other Shopping Ideas

Glassware
Duralex, Luminarc and Cristal D'Arques are names you may already be familiar with. They are available in the hypermarkets at prices that are at least 20% less than in the UK. You can visit **Cristal d'Arques'** factory at Zone Industrielle, RN43 Arques 62510, Tel: 00 33 321 93 46 96 (A26 motorway, Arques exit). There is a museum and a visitor centre and shop. Prices are generally 20% less than the French retail outlets, but call in advance. The visit costs around £3.00 and includes a gift.

Lace (Dentelles)
One of the local industries of Calais is lace making. The French take their lace so seriously that there is a museum dedicated to lace in Calais. Lace in France is not always cheaper, but you do get a wider choice. Look out for the specialist lace shops called dentellières.

Batteries
Around 20% cheaper in the hypermarkets.

Light Bulbs
Not a huge saving to be made, but 15% is enough to bring a little light.

Tissues
Both boxed and handbag size are at least 25% cheaper across the board.

Beauty Creams
Women's facial beauty creams tend to be a little cheaper in France. For instance a 100ml tube of Nivea cream costs £1.37 in France and £1.85 in the UK. Or Garnier Synergie Express 3 in 1 costs £2.62 in France and £2.85 in the UK. A range of Clarins products is also cheaper:
Clarins Cleansing Milk 200ml costs £8.09 (UK£13); 100ml Clarins Hand and Nail treatment cream costs £8.80 (UK£14); clarins Exfoliating Body Scrub 50ml costs £15.50 (UK£20).

Perfumes
French hypermarkets stock top-notch perfume which tend to be cheaper to buy in France. For instance Anais Anais Natural Spray is £22.65 (£28 UK), Calvin klein Eternity Spray is £28 (UK35).

Other Shopping Ideas

Mountain Bikes (VTT)

Although we are unable to give a true comparison on mountain bikes, we can say that the hypermarkets do have good value ones. Adult mountain bikes start at under £100 and children's mountain bikes can be found for around £40. It is difficult to find these prices in UK.

Garden Furniture (Jardinage)

Garden furniture is often half the UK price of the equivalent and tempting to buy - but you will need a lot of space in your car! At Leroy Merlin (next to Auchan), Continent, Carrefour and Auchan there is a good selection of both plastic and pine table and chair sets. Plastic chairs start from £2.50 and plastic tables 85cm in diameter from as little as £14.90. A pine table and chair set can be found for only £75.00.

Garden parasols are also around £10.00 cheaper in France.

Pots and Pans

You may already be familiar with the names Le Creuset and Tefal. These two popular quality brands of pots and pans are both manufactured in France. You can purchase these in the hypermarkets and supermarkets for as little as half the UK price. For example, the Le Creuset 20cm saucepan is typically sold in the UK for around £33.00 yet it is available at French hypermarkets at around £15.50.

Baby's Furniture

Furniture for babies is considerably less in france:

Prams -	25% less
High chairs -	25% less
Bouncy chairs -	35% less
Travel cots -	50% less
Car seats -	55% less

Other Shopping Ideas

TIP:
Serious bargain hunters should time their trip with the French sales. These happen twice a year - in January and in August and generally last between one to two months. You can pick up some fantastic bargains!

TIP:
In August, Calais becomes a huge outdoor flea market known as the Braderie - a great place to find a bargain.

TIP:
Take a cooler bag with you just in case you want to buy fresh products such as cheese or fish to maintain freshness and avoid any pungent smells on the journey home.

Tip:
Shops close at lunch time.

Tip:
Cat food, baked beans, tomato ketchup, sliced bread, margarine, tuna, frozen pizza, air freshener, nappies and most branded soap are actually more expensive in France!

Other Types of Shops on the High Street

Alimentation Général:
General store

Pharmacie:
Chemist that sells primarily medicines

Droguerie:
Related to the hardware store, selling primarily toiletries

Nettoyage à sec:
Dry cleaners

Carrelages
Sells tiles

Tabac:
Tobacconist cum newsagent that sells cigarettes and tobacco. Also sells stamps.

Maison de la Presse
Sells magazines and newspapers

Librairie:
Book shop

Quincaillerie:
Hardware store

Eating Out

In the Middle Ages, English soldiers pillaged the Artois countryside. But they stopped for lunch only to be horrified by the French cuisine. It was they who nicknamed the French "Frogs".

You know lunchtime has arrived in France when you see the sign 'fermé' (closed) on shop doors. As the shops and factories close, the restaurants open for business offering a mix of cuisine and ambience.

French culinary diversity is very much inspired by the country's variety of landscape and locally farmed produce.

Generally 3 distinct styles of cuisine are evident:

Haute Cuisine
The hallmarks of Haute Cuisine are its rich food and elaborate presentation. This style can be tracked back to Louis XIV's 12-hour feasts in the Palace of Versailles.

Cuisine Bourgeoise
This style is related to Haute Cuisine. Less elaborate perhaps and best described as high quality home cooking.

Nouvelle Cuisine
This trendy cooking style originated in the 1970s. The dishes are generally less rich, fresh ingredients are used and vegetables are al dente - almost raw - to optimise their natural flavours and aromas.

Which Restaurant?
Choosing a restaurant is easy as restaurants generally display their menus outside. Steer clear of empty restaurants - in our experience, they generally deserve to be so! If you have booked a table be sure to be on time, as it

is unlikely to be saved for more than ten minutes, especially on Sundays when everyone likes to eat out *en famille*.

Most restaurants cater for tourists by offering a *menu touristique* usually written in English or with an English translation alongside regional dishes.

This is often good value for money and comprises such dishes as steak and French fries.

One item that will be missing from any French menu is the traditional two-slices-of-bread British sandwich. You may find the term *sandwich* referred to on the menu at cafés or brasseries, but it will never be served in sliced bread.

The most popular *sandwich* is the croque monsieur which comprises ham and cheese in a ficelle (a slimmer version of a baguette). The feminine version of this is croque madame served with a fried egg too.

Alternatively, you could choose the Prix Fixe menu, a set price menu which may include the plât du jour (dish of the day) or spécialité de la maison (house special). These are a better choice for those wishing to try a local dish, usually seafood or frogs' legs, *cuisses de grenouilles*.

Indulge in the à la carte menu or the menu gastronomique for finer quality food.

Not all prices will be highlighted on the menu. The letters SG may sit alongside some dishes and stand for *selon grosseur* (according to weight). This applies to dishes that, for practical purposes, are sold by weight, such as lobster or fish. In this instance it is advisable to find out the price before you order.

If the words *service compris* (service included) or service et taxes compris (service and taxes included) are on the menu, then prices include a service charge. However, odd coins are usually left for the waiter. Otherwise, a 10% tip is customary.

Meals are never rushed in restaurants even a snack and a drink at one of the cafés. You can while away the time at your leisure but if you are eating to a deadline, pay for your meal when it arrives, as catching the waiter's eye later may prove a challenge.

Finally, it's worth noting that Everything has its time and place in France and that includes lunchtime.

In France restaurants are strictly open for lunch only between 12noon - 3pm. If you are in need of

sustenance outside these hours look for those restaurants that advertise that they are a **"non-stop"** restaurant, or approach a fritterie.

Otherwise you have no choice but to wait until the evening when the restaurants open again at around 7pm.

Alternative eateries to consider are the crêperies which tend to stay open all day; or even though it seems incongruous with French cuisine, in desparation you could head for a McDonald's for immediate relief or nip into a bar for a drink and hope they serve snacks.

Eating Out

Make no mistake...
a steak is rare
whichever way you ask for it!

Like most nations, France is peopled with carnivores. There is nothing unusual in that. But, it helps to know that when it comes to steak, the meat is invariably served rare.

The concept of medium or well done is not one easily understood by the typical French chef; he is more comfortable preparing the steak in differing degrees of rare. The reason for this is found in the national belief that the meat is more tender, tastier and better for the health if served rare.

If ordering steak in a restaurant, you will generally be asked if you like your steak **saignant** or **à point**. If neither appeal, you will have to be assertive and asked for it to be **bien, bien cuit** and hope for a medium done steak.

Steak terms:

Bleue
The meat has been cooked for barely two minutes and the meat has vaguely changed colour.

Saignant
The meat has been cooked for two or more minutes but the meat is still 'bleeding' red juices.

A Point
Considered medium done in France, but in truth the meat is rare.

Bien Cuit
This means well done in France, but in truth the steak is rare verging on medium.

Steak Tartare
Raw minced beef thoroughly mixed together with a raw egg yolk.

Eating Out

Tip: Go for French food while in France. This not only adds to the French experience, but also makes good economic sense; traditional British food and drink such as tea, Scotch whisky and gin or a plate of bacon and eggs are expensive. So check out the menu or tarif des consommations (if in a café or bar) for something that tickles your palate and accompany it with wine (vin ordinaire) or draught beer (pression).

French spirits and soft drinks are generally an inexpensive relative to their British counterparts on the menu.

Tip: To get the attention of the waiter lift your index finger and call Monsieur - not garçon (which will be ignored). A waitress should be addressed as Madame or Mademoiselle.

Tip: Do not ask for a doggy bag. This concept simply does not exist in France.

Tip: When ordering coffee, be specific and say exactly what you would like.

Unlike British restaurants, just ordering a coffee will not do because the French have a different idea of how it should be served. They will serve coffee strong and black, espresso style as standard. The exception to this is during the breakfast meal when coffee is served in large wide-mouthed coffee cups - specially designed for dunking - and milk is a standard accompaniment.

Coffee Styles

Un café, s'il vous plaît
You will receive an espresso coffee, strong and black in a small espresso cup

Un café au lait, s'il vous plaît
You will receive an espresso coffee with milk on the side.

Une crème s'il vous plaît
You will receive a small white coffee

Une crème grande s'il vous plaît
You will receive a white coffee served in a normal size cup.

Menu Reader

Terms on a French Menu

Le Viandes	Meat	Les Poissons	Fish
L'Agneau	Lamb	Anchois	Anchovy
Assiette	Plate of	Anguille	Eel
Anglaise	cold meats	Araignée	Spider Crab
Bifteck	Steak	L'Assiette	Smoked Fish
Bifteck Haché	Hamburger	Nordique	Platter
Boeuf	Beef	Bar et Loup de	
Carré d'Agneau	Rib of Lamb	Mer	Sea-wolf
Chevreuil	Venison	Barbe	Brill
Côtes	Lamb	Bigorneau	Winkle
d'Agneau	Chops	Cabillaud	Fresh Cod
Côte de Boeuf	Side of Beef	Carrelet et Plie	Plaice
Côte de Porc	Pork Chop	Colin	Hake
Côte de Veau	Veal	Coquilles St-	
Contrefilet	Sirloin	Jacques	Scallops
Entrecôte	Steak	Crabes	Crabs
Faux Filet	Sirloin Steak	Crevette Grise	Shrimp
Filet de Boeuf	Fillet of Beef	Crustacés	Shellfish
Foie	Liver	Dorade	Sea Bream
Foie de Veau	Calves' Liver	Ecrevisses	Crayfish
Gigot d'Agneau	Leg of Lamb	Escargots	Snails
Jambon	Ham	Etrille	Swimming Crab
Langue	Tongue	Fruit de Mer	Seafood
Langue de Boeuf	Ox Tongue	Gamba	Large Prawn
Lapin	Rabbit	Harengs	Herring
Lard Fumé	Smoked Bacon	Homard	Lobster
Lièvre	Hare	Limande	Lemon Sole
Porc	Pork	Langouste	Spiny Lobster
Rognons	Kidneys	Langoustines	Norway Lobster
Saucisse	Sausage	Huître	Oyster
Tête de Veau	Calves' Head	Lieu	Coal Fish

Menu Reader

Les Poissons / **Fish contd.**

Limande	Lemon Sole
Maquereau	Mackerel
Merlan	Whiting
Morue	Cod
Moules	Mussels
Péntoncle	Small Scallop
Praire	Clam
Raie	Skate
Rouget	Red Mullet
Salad Océan	Ocean Salad
Sardines	Sardines
Saumon	Salmon
Sole	Sole
Thon	Tuna
Truite (de Mer)	Trout (Sea)
Truite arc en ciel	Rainbow Trout
Turbot	Turbot

Volaille / **Poultry**

Caneton/Canard	Duck
Caille	Quail
Dindon	Turkey
Oie	Goose
Faisan	Pheasant
Foie Gras	Duck Liver pâté
Foie Volaille	Chicken Liver
Lotte	Monkfish
Magret Canard	Duck Fillet
Perdreau	Partridge
Pigeon	Pigeon
Poulet	Chicken
Poularde	Boiled Chicken
Poussin	Spring Chicken
Ris de Veau	Veal sweetbread

Sauce / **Sauce**

Béarnaise	Sauce made from egg yolks, shallots, wine and tarragon
Béchamel	White sauce with herbs
Beurre Blanc	Loire sauce with butter, wine and shallots
Beurre Noir	Blackened butter
Meunière	Butter and lemon sauce

How do you like your eggs?

Oeufs	Eggs
- Coque	- Boiled
- Brouillés	- Scrambled
- Pochés	- Poached
Oeufs sur le plat	Fried eggs

Menu Reader

A-Z of Miscellaneous French Menu Terms

Abricots	Apricots	Cresson	Cress
Amandes	Almonds	Croustade	Tartlets
Ananas	Pineapple	Cuit au Four	Baked
Araignée	Spider-crab	Endives	Chicory
Artichaut	Artichoke	Epinards	Spinach
Asperge	Asparagus	Estragon	Tarragon
Aubergines	Aubergines	Farine	Flour
Avocat	Avocado	Fenouil	Fennel
Bécasse	Woodcock	Fèves	Beans
Betteraves	Beetroot	Figues	Figs
Beurre	Butter	Flageolets	Kidney Beans
Braisé	Braised	Fraises	Strawberry
Brochette	Skewer	Framboises	Raspberries
Brouillade	Stew with oil	Fromage Blanc	Cream Cheese
Caille	Quail	Fromage Chèvre	Goats' Cheese
Carottes	Carrots	Fromages	Cheeses
Céleri	Celery	Fumé	Smoked
Cerises	Cherries	Gratinée	Grill browned
Champignons	Mushrooms	Grenouilles	Frogs
Châtaignes	Chestnuts	Grillé	Grilled
Chicorée	Chicory	Groseilles	Currants
Choux Bruxelle	Brussel Sprout	Harricots Verts	French Beans
Chou Rouge	Red Cabbage	Laitue	Lettuce
Chou vert	Kale	Mais	Sweet Corn
Choux Fleurs	Cauliflowers	Mandarines	Mandarines
Citron	Lemon	Marron	Chestnut
Concombre	Cucumber	Melon	Melon
Consommé	Clear soup	Navets	Turnips
Courgettes	Courgette	Noisettes	Hazelnuts
Crème Glacée	Ice cream	Noix	Walnuts
Crêpes	Pancakes		

Menu Reader

Oie	Goose
Oignons	Onions
Oseille	Sorrel
Oursins	Sea Hedgehog
Pastèque	Water Melon
Pêches	Peaches
Petits Pois	Green Peas
Pintade	Guinea-fowl
Pissenlits	Dandelions
Poire	Pear
Poivre	Pepper
Poireaux	Leeks
Poivrons rouges	Red Pepper
Poivrons Verts	Green Pepper
Pomme de Terre	Potato
Pomme	Apple
Potage	Soup
Prunes	Prunes
Radis	Radishes
Railfort	Horse Radish
Raisins	Grapes
Reine-Claude	Greengages
Riz	Rice
Rôti	Roasted
Sel	Salt
Supréme	Chicken breast or game bird
Tomates	Tomatoes
Terrine	Coarse paté

Some dishes you might see on a menu in northern France:

Waterzoi
A variety of fish in a lush, creamy sauce

Soupe de poissons
Fish soup

Rognon de veau rôti
Roasted veal kidney

Ris de veau pêle
Fried veal sweetbread

Faux filet de boeuf
Sirloin steak

Filet de haren mariné
Marinated herring

Carré d'agneau
Loin of lamb

Courses on the Menu

Apéritif A predinner drink
Hors d'Oeuvre Cold and/or warm snacks taken before the main meal
Entrée First course/starter
Plat principal. Main course
Salade A simple green salad
Dessert Dessert
Café Coffee
Digestif After dinner drink

Choosing Hotels

Check Out the Automatic Check-Inns

If you are looking to stay overnight or longer on a budget then any of France's budget hotels may be a good option. For these hotels, functionality is the primary concern, so no room service, luxurious towels, beautiful furniture or scenic views. But they are usually situated close to the motorway networks, so you can check in and out and be back on route with ease.

These hotels operate on an unmanned auto-check-in basis. Entrance is by credit card through a "hole in the wall" using the language of your choice, and offer 24-hour access. The rooms are clean, functional and usually comprise a double and a single bed (bunk) plus a colour TV.

The Formule 1 hotel is cheap at around £19 per night for up to three people but the shower and toilet is communal - most annoying if you get into the shower only to find you have forgotten the soap!

Restaurants are never part of the internal landscape of a budget hotel, but there is always an accessible snack vending machine. In the morning a simple continental breakfast, though not cordon bleu, is good value for money at around £2.50 per person.

The majority of hotels in France are one and two star

BUDGET HOTELS IN FRANCE			
Type	Room price from £	Beds/ room	Central Reservation
B&B	16.00	4	00 33 2 98 33 75 00
Bonsai	15.00	3	00 33 1 42 46 15 45
Formule 1	13.00	3	00 33 8 36 68 56 85
Mister Bed	15.00	4	00 33 1 46 14 38 00

Choosing Hotels

hotels and prices tend to vary depending on location and comfort. The chain hotels can generally be relied upon to deliver a good quality of service within their star rating. For instance, you can expect a TV, telephone and an en-suite shower room as part of the package in a two star hotel. A bathroom would cost more.

Chambres d'hôtes are becoming popular in France.These are French style bed and breakfasts, mostly run by ordinary people who have turned their private homes into tourist accommodation. They tend to be cheaper than hotels and give a flavour of French life and character. Breakfast tends to be just a coffee, bread or croissant and maybe cheese. These days, many B&B signs offer an English breakfast and this is testament to the increasing number of British visitors.

A gîte - lodging - situated in the countryside gives a feeling of rural living. The kind of accommodation ranges from a simple room or perhaps an entire house.

Contact Gîtes de France for more information on 00 33 1 47 42 20 20.

Châteaux also make for beautiful retreats and are often old castles or country mansions found mainly in rural areas.

1 & 2 STAR HOTEL CHAINS IN FRANCE	
Tariffs vary between £20-£60 per room	
Name	Central Reservation
Balladins *	00 33 1 64 46 49 00
Campanile - Motel style	00 33 1 64 62 46 46
Ibis-Arcade **	00 33 1 69 91 05 63
Logis de France * / ** / ***	00 33 1 45 84 83 84

Driving in France

Driving along the well-maintained roads and motorways in France is a pleasure. But be sure not to break the law.

En Route:
To comply with French motoring regulations, please note what is and is not essential:

It is essential:
- To have a full UK driving licence and all motoring documents.
- To be over the age of 18 - even if you have passed your test in the UK.
- Not to exceed 90km/h in the first year after passing your test.
- To display a GB sticker or Euro number plate.
- To carry a red warning triangle.
- To wear rear and front seat belts.
- To affix headlamp diverters. These are widely available in motoring shops or DIY with black masking tape.

It is not essential:
- To have a green card although very helpful.
- To have yellow headlights.

Traffic News:
Tune in to Autoroute FM107.7 for French traffic news in English and French.

Speed Limits
In France speed limits are shown in kilometres per hour **not** miles per hour. Always adhere to these speed limits as in France they are strictly enforced:

	MPH	km/h
Toll motorways	81	130
Dual Carriageways	69	110
Other Roads	55	90
Towns	31	50

When raining, these speed limits are reduced by 6mph on the roads and 12mph on the motorway. In fog, speed is restricted to 31mph. As well as speed traps, it is useful to know that entrance and exit times through the toll booths can be checked on your toll ticket and may be used as evidence of speeding!

Driving in France

Motorways & Roads:
French motorways (autoroutes) are marked by blue and white A signs. Many motorways are privately owned and outside towns a toll charge (péage) is usually payable and can be expensive. This can be paid by credit card (Visa Card, Eurocard, Mastercard), or euros at automatic gates, so be prepared. Contact a tourist board for the exact cost. if you have access to the internet click on **www.autoroutes.fr.**

Roads are indicated as:

A roads -
Autoroutes - Motorways where a toll is probably payable.

N Roads -
routes nationales - toll free, single lane roads. Slower than A roads.

D roads -
Routes départementales - scenic alternatives to A roads.

C roads -
routes communales - country roads.

Roadside Messages:
For safety's sake, it is very important to be aware of the roadside messages:

Carrefour   Crossroad
Déviation   Diversion
Priorité à droite
Give way to traffic on the right
Péage   Toll
Ralentir   Slow down
Vous n'avez pas la priorité
           Give way
Rappel   Restriction continues
Sens unique   One way
Serrez à droite/   Keep right/
à gauche   Keep left
Véhicules lents
          Slow vehicles
Gravillons   Loose chippings
Chaussée Déformée
 Uneven road and temporary surface
Nids de Poules   Potholes

Drink Driving:
French law dictates that a 50g limit of alcohol is allowed - just one glass of wine. Exceed this limit and you risk confiscation of your licence, impounding of the car, a prison sentence or an on-the-spot fine between £20 to £3,000!

Driving in France

Tyre Pressure:
It is crucial to ensure that your tyres are at the correct pressure to cater for heavy loads. Make sure you do not exceed the car's maximum carrying weight. The following table gives a guide to typical loads:

| 1 case of | Qty | Weight | |
		kg	lbs
Wine	x 2	15kg	33lbs
Champagne	x12	22kg	48lbs
Beer 25cl	x 2	8kg	18lbs

Filling Up:
To fill up, head for petrol stations attached to the hypermarkets as these offer the best value fuel. Petrol stations on the motorway - autoroutes - tend to be more expensive. Though sterling and travellers cheques are not accepted, credit cards usually are. Some petrol stations have automated payment facilities by credit card. These are generally 24 hour petrol stations and tend to be unmanned in the evening but do not rely on them for fuel salvation as they often do not accept international credit cards!

Currently petrol and diesel are cheaper in France.

Petrol grades are as follows:

Unleaded petrol -
l'essence sans plomb. Available in 95 & 98 grades - equates to UK premium and super grades respectively.

Leaded petrol -
l'essence or Super
Graded as:
90 octane (2 star),
93 octane (3 star)
97 octane (4 star).
Gazole - Diesel Fuel
GPL - LPG (liquefied petroleum gas)

IMPORTANT!

- IF THERE ARE NO STOP SIGNS AT THE INTERSECTION, CARS MUST YIELD TO THE RIGHT

- CHILDREN UNDER 10 ARE NOT ALLOWED TO TRAVEL IN THE FRONT

- DRIVE ON THE RIGHT, OVERTAKE ON THE LEFT

Driving in France

Breakdown on Motorways:
If you should break down on the motorway and you do not have breakdown cover, **DON'T PANIC**, you can still get assistance. There are emergency telephones stationed every mile and a half on the motorway. These are directly linked to the local police station. The police are able to locate you automatically and arrange for an approved repair service to come to your aid.

Naturally there is a cost for this and fees are regulated. Expect to pay around £50 for labour plus parts and around £55 for towing.
An extra 25% supplement is also charged if you break down between 6pm and 8am and any time on Saturdays, Sundays and national holidays.

At the garage, ensure you ask for un Ordre de Réparation (repair quote) which you should sign. This specifies the exact nature of the repairs, how long it will take to repair your vehicle and, importantly, the cost!

Emergency Phrases:

Please, help
Aidez-moi s'il vous plaît

My car has broken down
Ma voiture est en panne

I have run out of petrol
Je suis en panne d'essence

The engine is overheating
Le moteur surchauffe

There is a problem with the brakes
Il y a un problème de freins

I have a flat tyre
J'ai un pneu crevé

The battery is flat
La batterie est vide

There is a leak in the petrol tank/in the radiator
Il y a une fuite dans le réservoir d'essence/dans le radiateur

Can you send a mechanic/breakdown van?
Pouvez-vous envoyer un mécanicien/une dépanneuse?

Can you tow me to a garage?
Pouvez-vous me remorquer jusqu'à un garage?

I have had an accident
J'ai eu un accident

The windscreen is shattered
Le pare-brise est cassé

Call an ambulance
Appelez une ambulance

Accidents:

If you do have an accident you must fill out a damage assessment form. Get this from your insurance company before you leave. It must be signed by the other party and in the event of a dispute or a refusal to complete the form you should immediately obtain a constat d'huissier. This is a written report from a bailiff (huisser). In the event of a dispute call the police so that you can make out an official report. If someone is injured call the SAMU (15) or the fire brigade (18). The police are only called out to accidents when someone is injured or a driver is under the influence of alcohol or the accident impedes the flow of traffic.

Parking:

Illegal parking in France can be penalised by a fine, wheel clamping or vehicle removal. Park wherever you see a white dotted line or if there are no markings at all.

There are also numerous pay and display meters. (horodateurs) where small change is required to buy a ticket. The ticket should be displayed inside the car windscreen on the driver's side.

If you find a blue parking zone (zone bleue), this will be indicated by a blue line on the pavement or road and a blue signpost with a white letter P. If there is a square under the P then you have to display a cardboard disc which has various times on it. They allow up to two and a half hours parking time. The discs are available in supermarkets or petrol stations and are sometimes given away free. Ask for a **disque de stationnement.**

Services:

On the motorways every

10km	rest areas for short stops
40km	service stations and restaurants
100+km	motels for overnight stops

Money Matters

Currency:
The currency used in France is the Euro. This is made up of notes and Euror coins and cents.

When you are looking at a price tag, menu or receive a receipt be aware that unlike the British system of separating pounds and pence with a decimal point, in France there is no decimal point, Euros and cents are separated by a comma.

Unlimited currency may be taken into France but you must declare bank notes of 50,000 Euros or more if you are bringing this back.

Currency Exchange:
Changing money from sterling to Euros can be expensive. Use your credit card to pay for goods abroad, as credit card companies give a better rate of exchange and do not charge commission when buying goods abroad. Of course you will require some cash. Change your money in

the UK where it can be a little more competitive than in France.

In France you can also change money and cash travellers cheques at the post office (PTT), banks, stations and private bureaux de change. You can also make a purchase in the hypermarkets in Calais in sterling, as change is given in Euros without commission. Though convenient, always be aware of the exchange rate. Some shops do take advantage.

Travellers cheques can be used as cash and if you wish to turn them into cash at a French bank you will receive the face value - no commission.

Most banks in France do not accept Eurocheques

Credit Cards:
Credit cards are widely accepted To use your credit card ensure that you have your passport handy as you may be expected to produce it. If your card has been

Money Matters

rejected in a shop or restaurant, it could be that their card reading machine does not recognise it - some French credit cards have a 'puce', a microchip with security information on it. British cards do not. French tourist authorities recommend you say:

Les cartes anglaises ne sont pas des cartes à puce, mais à band magnétique. Ma carte est valable et je vous serais reconnaissant d'en demander la confirmation auprès de votre banque ou de votre centre de traitement.'

which means:
English cards don't have an information chip, but a magnetic band. My card is valid and I would be grateful if you would confirm this with your bank or processing centre.'

If you need to contact
Barclaycard
Tel: +44 (0)1604 234234

Visa
Tel: +44 (0)1383 621166

Visa in France
Tel: 01 45 67 84 84

Cashpoints:
You can use your cashpoint card to get local currency from cash-dispensing machines. This service is available at major banks such as: Crédit Lyonnais, Crédit Agricole and Crédit Mutuel. If the machine bears the same logo as that displayed on your card, such as Visa or Delta, then you can insert your card and follow the instructions. These are likely to be in English as your card will be recognised as British. Punch in your PIN and press the button marked **Envoi.** When prompted tell the machine how much you want in French francs. You will see phrases such as:

Tapez votre code secret - Enter your pin
Veuillez patienter - Please wait
Opération en cours - Money on its way!

Out and About in France

Shopping:

Shops and supermarkets open and close as follows:

Open	9.00 am
Close lunch-time	12.00 noon
Open again	2.00 pm
Close finally	5.00-7.00 pm

Most shops are closed on Sunday and some on Monday. Supermarket trolleys (les chariots) require a (refundable) 1 euro piece.

Taxi!

It is cheaper to hail a taxi in the street or cab ranks indicated by the letter 'T' than order one by telephone. This is because a telephone-requested taxi will charge for the time taken to reach you. Taxi charges are regulated. The meter must show the minimum rate on departure and the total amount (tax included) on arrival.

If the driver agrees that you share the taxi, he has the right to turn the meter back to zero at each stop showing the minimum charge again.

A tip *(pourboire)* is expected. It is customary to pay 10-15%.

Public Holidays:

Most French shops will be shut on the following days:

Jan 1	New Year	Jour de l'an
Apr*	Easter Monday	Lundi de Pâques
May 1	Labour Day	Fête du Travail
May 8	Victory Day	Armistice 1945
May*	Ascension	Ascension
May*	Whitsun	Lundi de Pentecôte
July 14	Bastille Day	Fête nationale
Aug 15	Assumption	Assomption
Nov 1	All Saints'	Toussaint
Nov 11	Armistice Day	Armistice 1918
Dec 25	Christmas	Noël

*Dates change each year.

Tipping:

Tipping is widely accepted in France. However, restaurant menus with the words 'servis compris' indicate that service is included but small change can be left if so desired. The following is the accepted norm for tipping:

Restaurants service usually included	Optional
Cafés service usually included	Optional
Hotels	No
Hairdressers	2 euros
Taxis	2 euros
Porters	2 euros
Cloakroom attendants	Small change
Toilets	Small change

Caught on the Hop!

Cafés allow you to use their toilets for free. Shopping centres also have facilities. If you see a white saucer, place a coin or two in it. In the streets you may see the Sanisette, a white cylindrical building. Insert the required coin in the slot to open the door. After use the Sanisette scrubs itself.

No Smoking!

It is forbidden to smoke in public places. However, there are quite often spaces reserved in cafés and restaurants for smokers.

Pharmacy:

These are recognised by their green cross sign. Staff tend to be highly qualified so are able to give medical advice on minor ailments, provide first aid and prescribe some drugs. Some drugs are only available via a doctor's prescription (ordonnance).

Doctor:

Any pharmacy will have an address of a doctor. Consultation fees are generally about £15.00.

Ask for a Feuille de Soins (Statement of Treatment) if you are insured.

Medical Aid:

As members of the EU, the British can get urgent medical treatment in France at reduced costs on production of a form E111 available from the Department of Health and Social Security. A refund can then be obtained in person or by post from the local Social Security Offices (Caisse Primaire d'Assurance Maladie).

Electricity:

You will need a continental adapter plug (with round pins). The voltage in France is 220V and 240V in the UK.

Television/Video Tapes:

French standard TV broadcast system is SECAM whereas in the UK it is PAL. Ordinary video cassettes bought in France will show only in black and white. French video tapes cannot be played on British videos. Ask for VHS PAL system.

Out and About in France

Phoning Home:
Phonecards (Télécartes) are widely used and available at travel centres, post offices, tobacconists and shops displaying the Télécarte sign.

Cheap rate (50% extra time) is between 22.30hrs-08.00hrs Monday to Friday, 14.00hrs-08.00hrs Saturday, all day Sunday & public holidays. To call the UK dial 00, at the dialling tone dial 44 followed by the phone number and omit 0 from the STD code.

Writing Home:
Post offices (PTT) are open Monday to Friday during office hours and half day on Saturday. Smaller branches tend to close between noon and 2pm. Stamps can also be bought from tobacconists.

The small but bright yellow post boxes are easy to spot.

What's the Time?
French summer starts on the last Sunday in March at 2am and ends on the last Sunday in October at 3am. Time is based on Central European Time (Greenwich Mean Time + 1 hour in winter and + 2 hours in summer). France is one hour ahead. The clocks are put forward 1 hour in the spring and put back 1 hour in the autumn.

Passports:
Before travelling to France you need a full 10- year British passport. Non--British nationals require a visa and regulations vary according to your nationality. Contact the French Consulate.

Pet Passports:
Since 28th February 2000, a scheme has been in force enabling cats and dogs to travel abroad without being subjected to six months quarantine. A blood test is required and a microchip is fitted. Not more than 48 hours before return, the animal must be treated for tics and tapeworms. Only then will it be awarded the official pet passport'. Further information is available from PETS helpline 0870 2411 710.

Conversion Tables

What's Your Size?
When buying clothes in France, check the conversion tables below to find out your size

Women's Shoes

GB		FR			FR
3	=	$35^1/_2$	$5^1/_2$	=	39
$3^1/_2$	=	36	6	=	$39^1/_2$
4	=	37	$6^1/_2$	=	40
$4^1/_2$	=	$37^1/_2$	7	=	$40^1/_2$
5	=	38	8	=	$41^1/_2$

Women's Dresses/Suits

GB		FR	GB		FR
8	=	36	14	=	42
10	=	38	16	=	44
12	=	40	18	=	46

Women's Blouses/Sweaters

GB		FR	GB		FR
30	=	36	36	=	42
32	=	38	38	=	44
34	=	40	40	=	46

Men's Shirts

GB		FR	GB		FR
$14^1/_2$ =		37	16	=	41
15	=	38	$16^1/_2$ =		42
$15^1/_2$ =		39/40	17	=	43

Men's Suits

GB		FR	GB		FR
36	=	46	42	=	52
38	=	48	44	=	54
40	=	50	46	=	56

Men's Shoes

GB		FR	GB		FR
7	=	40	10	=	43
8	=	41	11	=	44
9	=	42	12	=	45
			13	=	46

Weights and Measures:

Distance 1.6 km	=	1 mile
Weight 1 kg	=	2.20lbs
Liquid 4.54 litres	=	1 gallon
Liquid 1 litre	=	1.76 pints
Length 1m	=	39.37inches
Area 1sq metre	=	1.196 sq yds

Speed

kpm	mph	kpm	mph
50	31	100	62
70	43	110	68
80	50	120	75
90	56	130	81

How Much Can You Bring Back?

In theory there are no limits on the amount of alcohol or tobacco for personal use.
In practice exceeding the Advisory Guidelines, means you could be stopped

Since 1st January 1993, you are permitted to bring back as much alcohol and tobacco as you like, but it must be for personal use only. So you can happily stock up for Christmas or parties or weddings.

Although H. M. Customs and Excise have no authority to limit the amount you bring back into this country they do have the right to stop you if your purchases exceed the Advisory Guidelines. In this case you may be required to prove that the goods are for your own personal use. That means you cannot buy goods on behalf of anyone else, even your own mother!

If you are stopped, remember that the H.M. Customs officer is looking for bootleggers or those intent on resale. Other products such as mineral water, or any other non-alcoholic or food products, are not limited in any way.

Enjoy.

Advisory Guidelines
as set by H.M. Customs & Excise

Wine	90 litres
Spirits	10 litres
Fortified wine	20 litres
Beer	110 litres
Cigarettes	3200
Cigars	200
Cigarillos	400
Tobacco	3 kilogram

Note: People under 17 are not allowed to bring in tobacco and alcohol

Quick Currency Converter £ to Euro

£	@ 1.60	£	@ 1.60	£	@ 1.60	£	@ 1.60
0.10	0.16	21.00	33.60	69.00	110.40	117.00	187.20
0.20	0.32	22.00	35.30	70.00	112.00	118.00	188.80
0.30	0.48	23.00	36.80	71.00	113.60	119.00	190.40
0.40	0.64	24.00	38.40	72.00	115.20	120.00	192.00
0.50	0.80	25.00	40.00	73.00	116.80	121.00	193.60
0.60	0.96	26.00	41.60	74.00	118.40	122.00	195.20
0.63	1.00	27.00	43.20	75.00	120.00	123.00	196.90
0.70	1.12	28.00	44.80	76.00	121.60	124.00	198.40
0.80	1.28	29.00	46.40	77.00	123.20	125.00	200.00
0.90	1.44	30.00	48.00	78.00	124.80	126.00	201.60
1.00	1.60	31.00	49.60	79.00	126.40	127.00	203.20
1.50	2.40	32.00	51.20	80.00	128.00	128.00	204.80
2.00	3.20	33.00	52.80	81.00	129.60	129.00	206.40
2.50	4.00	34.00	54.40	82.00	131.20	130.00	208.00
3.00	4.80	35.00	56.00	83.00	132.80	131.00	209.60
3.50	5.60	36.00	57.60	84.00	134.40	132.00	211.20
4.00	6.40	37.00	59.20	85.00	136.00	133.00	212.80
4.50	7.20	38.00	60.80	86.00	137.60	134.00	214.40
5.00	8.00	39.00	62.40	87.00	139.20	135.00	216.00
5.50	8.80	40.00	64.00	88.00	140.80	136.00	217.60
6.00	9.60	41.00	65.60	89.00	142.40	137.00	219.20
6.50	10.40	42.00	67.20	90.00	144.00	138.00	220.80
7.00	11.20	43.00	68.80	91.00	145.60	139.00	222.40
7.50	12.00	44.00	70.40	92.00	147.20	140.00	224.00
8.00	12.80	45.00	72.00	93.00	148.80	141.00	225.60
8.50	13.60	46.00	73.60	94.00	150.40	142.00	227.20
9.00	14.40	47.00	75.20	95.00	152.00	143.00	228.80
9.50	15.20	48.00	76.80	96.00	153.60	144.00	230.40
10.00	16.00	49.00	78.40	97.00	155.20	145.00	232.00
10.50	16.80	50.00	80.00	98.00	156.80	146.00	233.60
11.00	17.60	51.00	81.60	99.00	158.40	147.00	235.20
11.50	18.40	52.00	83.20	100.00	160.00	148.00	236.80
12.00	19.20	53.00	84.80	101.00	161.60	149.00	238.40
12.50	20.00	54.00	86.40	102.00	163.20	150.00	240.00
13.00	20.80	55.00	88.00	103.00	164.80	155.00	248.00
13.50	21.60	56.00	89.60	104.00	166.40	160.00	256.00
14.00	22.40	57.00	91.20	105.00	168.00	165.00	264.00
14.50	23.20	58.00	92.80	106.00	169.60	170.00	272.00
15.00	24.00	59.00	94.40	107.00	171.20	175.00	289.00
15.50	24.80	60.00	96.00	108.00	172.80	180.00	288.00
16.00	25.60	61.00	97.60	109.00	174.40	185.00	296.00
16.50	26.40	62.00	99.20	110.00	176.00	190.00	304.00
17.00	27.20	63.00	100.80	111.00	177.60	195.00	312.00
17.50	28.00	64.00	102.40	112.00	179.20	200.00	320.00
18.00	28.80	65.00	104.00	113.00	180.80	225.00	360.00
18.50	29.60	66.00	105.60	114.00	182.40	250.00	400.00
19.00	30.40	67.00	107.20	115.00	184.00	275.00	440.00
20.00	32.00	68.00	108.80	116.00	185.60	300.00	480.00

Carrefour Cité Europe

Everything you need under one roof
Calendar of big events for the year

February

All for The Baby

March

Whisky, Beer & Spring Wine Fare

April

Garden Chairs & Tables

May

Swimming Pool Equipment

June

All for The Barbecue

July

Summer Sales & Luggage

August

All for The Baby

September

Autumn Wine Fare

October

Carrefour's 40th Birthday

November

Christmas Chocolate
Traditional Beaujolais Red Wine

December

All For Christmas Celebrations

January 2004

Winter Sales

Carrefour us OE 5 Jus sys 100 1, Jeulsrood du Kuri 62223 J Os qualas Tel 0 3 21.4d.%b.bb Jus: 03.21.4d.%b.bY